77 B
4 -

LOVE IN THE GARDEN

LOVE IN THE GARDEN

JEAN-PIERRE OTTE

foreword by Jacques Lacarrière

translated from the French by

Moishe Black and Maria Green

GEORGE BRAZILLER / PUBLISHER

New York

The translators gratefully acknowledge the help of typist Kathleen Swann,
entomologist Donald Buckle, and copyists Geraldine Black and Martha Hollinger.

Originally published in France under the title *L'Amour au jardin*
by Éditions Phébus in 1995.

First published in the United States of America in 2000 by George Braziller, Inc.

Copyright © 1995 by Éditions Phébus

English translation copyright © 2000 by George Braziller, Inc.

For information, please address the publisher:

George Braziller, Inc.
171 Madison Avenue
New York, NY 10016

Library of Congress Cataloging-in-Publication Data:
Otte, Jean Pierre, 1949–
    [Amour au jardin. English]
    Love in the garden / by Jean-Pierre Otte ; foreword by Jacques Lacarrière ;
translated by Moishe Black and Maria Green.
        p. cm.
    ISBN 0-8076-1467-X
    I. Black, Moishe. II. Green, Maria. III. Title.

PQ2675.T8 A4613 2000
843'.914—dc21   00-029778

Design by Rita Lascaro

Printed and bound in the United States of America

FIRST EDITION

For my wife,

at once woman and garden,

"fruit with the flower still visible."

CONTENTS

FOREWORD

One of the first lessons to be learned from this book—and a simpler lesson would be hard to imagine—is the recognition of a very basic but neglected truth: humans couple whereas animals mate. "Much ado about nothing!" you may say. "Where's the difference?" The difference lies in a single but essential fact: humans are supposed to choose each other whereas animals are supposed to encounter each other. Conscious choice versus chance. I know this distinction can always be argued about, but the fact remains: the further up (or down) you go in the scale of living things, from the human to the animal and from the animal toward the plant, the more uncertain and chancy the modes of love, mating, and reproducing become. For instance, many plants—and notably the ones described in this book—require third-party intervention, by the wind or by insects, in order to reproduce. To entrust our seed to the wind (or confide it to the waves, as fishes do) in order to have a child, might be a very poetic deed, but a very sterile one. Yet for sea creatures, trees, and flowers, it works! Which, incidentally, suggests that Nature is highly optimistic, willing to bet against all odds that an insect will light on a particular flower at the right time and place and act out, unconsciously and unaware, its role as go-between, you might even say procurer!

So it is that a multitude of pairing-off rituals, mating habits, weddings, and nuptials, now sumptuous, now murderous, unfold in this book, which is a virtual compendium of garden-scented marital intimacy! For the book was written by a person who, like J. H. Fabre, has for years closely, in fact very closely, observed the lives of the flowers, insects, and animals in his garden and has contrived to go beyond mere descriptions, however precise and valuable those may be; a person who, like Lewis Carroll's Alice, has managed to pass through the invisible looking glass separating us from our floral and faunal fellow creatures.

The author invites us on a journey to the heart of calyxes and corollas, into the intimacy of saps and grasses, a journey that transforms us into voyeurs who are at first astonished, then delighted, enchanted, occasionally even horrified by these lovemakings that so often turn voracious. Reading *Love in the Garden*, I was reminded several times of Ernst Jünger's book *Subtle Hunts*, that extraordinary, teeming descent into the insect world of the Sardinian bushland. But Jean-Pierre Otte goes further: where Jünger stops cold at the forbidden threshold of that other world, J.-P. Otte keeps going, penetrating the boundless private world surrounding him. After all, doesn't he very rightly point out that "the boundless universe of anthills is easier for us to grasp than the boundless universe of the galaxies"? The result is that with Mr. Otte the spectator becomes an actor, the observer becomes an explorer, and the voyeur becomes the seer. Indeed, it takes a visionary to capture in words the anguish of an insect imprisoned in the venomous private parts of an arum plant, the intoxication of a bumblebee in the crimson crypts of a grape hyacinth, the ecstasy of slugs fused in piercing hermaphroditic embrace. "Anthropomorphism!" I hear you say. "The standard mistake made by all amateurs." Sometimes, admittedly, the author lets himself get carried away by the fun of putting an increasingly human spin on things, of moving from phasmids to fantasies, of coming daringly close to dragging the reader through a gallery of monsters with human faces. But at no point is there a break in his link with the merciless, demanding reality of the natural world, that extraordinary universe full of rustlings, matings, and movements of creatures devouring each other right on our human doorstep.

A universe, it should be added, composed mainly of lures, false appearances, masks, and shams in which branches can suddenly change place, or petals become silky bee bellies. A world resembling a mirror with implacable reflections that draw you inexorably closer and closer. But now someone has dared to step through the mirror, faithfully describing and reconstructing what he found. It had to be someone deeply and patiently versed in the secrets of the senses and the seasons, a gardener who, like Jean-Pierre Otte, toils in the garden of love.

—Jacques Lacarrière

I was

in many forms

before I was free.

—Taliesin

PART

I

The Astonishing Deception of the Bee Orchid

To be a bumblebee, or even a bumblebee drone, is to lead a fairly comfortable life with ordinary tasks that are clearly defined. That life does, however, have its share of surprises and perils, its weird and wonderful pitfalls, and its frustrations—frustrations that may be logical and necessary, but from the bee's point of view are baffling, incomprehensible, and unfair.

In order to do all the things they are called on to do, bees have to manage as best they can with a stout, heavy body, tightly laced into a tawny velvet corset, hooped in copper and vermilion, and epically hairy. Magnificent if somewhat protuberant black eyes take up and adorn almost the entire head.

When they emerge from the colony, temporarily free from the bustling social activity in which they represent merely one more winged organism, the bees fly off in their several directions, plunder or prurient-pleasure bound, but quite soon come away again, back to the teeming community, for numbers are their breath of life.

Their errands are always solitary, with no other accompaniment than the muffled, deep, continuous whir of their wings. The thousands of units that make up their multifaceted globular eyes construct a visual mosaic out of all they behold. Whatever way their gaze may turn, it finds a jigsaw puzzle with no missing pieces: cut up, fragmented, striated, but forming a perfect whole at all times. And should a ray of sunlight cross the flowery scene, it is as though a stained-glass window had suddenly caught fire, each segment shining within its slender, leaden ligatures.

The sorties these pilots fly are self-serving reconnaissance raids, liqueur-sampling pub crawls, silken revelings in corollas, wraparound romps in the tightly fitting pink petticoats of a poppy, break and entries through the intimacy of many a moist, translucent membrane. They venture into the secret paths of anthers, where the pollen masses are hid. With stiff and slightly hollowed tongue, they suck up the nectar, get drunk on the ambrosia of sage, violet, or monkshood, on the yellow wine of a linden flower. From bar to bar they fly, mixing new cocktails as they go, drunker yet and drunker, losing themselves in the satiny wine-stores and cellars.

And when it's time to make their way home, they fly a ponderous zigzag course. Laden with loot, senses dilated, and minds befuddled, they are repeatedly obliged to adjust for motor coordination disturbances; aerial drunks on a wavering low-altitude flight path, with their heads held down to spot the occasional familiar landmark. They might be so many fat, buzzing marbles wandering along, their bodies rubbed in sunshine, but not a hair out of place in their distinctive garb of gold and darkest brown.

One of them, a drone, is threading his way through the final drops of a spring shower. Beyond the rain, under the lake-blue patches of clear sky, he confronts a stretch of ground he doesn't know, an area he has in fact been over before, but suddenly unfamiliar with resplendent light. Mists are on the move, and a watery sheen has been added to the colors. Clumsily he goes along, tracing twists and turns, bends and meanders, veering off toward the heads of blossoming plants, doing whatever seems most likely to produce booty and the opportunity for some solo sousing. So far, he has stubbornly forced his way into a few corollas, but in every case others have been there before him. Others have looted the pollen lofts, and he notes where fragile blossoms have been ripped and torn.

He ventures farther, still farther, and still tacking like a drunken sailor, to places he has never been, into territory where nothing is familiar. And suddenly in a chance air current he detects the atoms of a potent perfume very like the one given off by a female of his own species. The smell, which there can be no mistaking, stretches out thin, breaks up, wanders off in all directions; he hunts till he finds the main thread again, backtracks, loses the trail in the astringent exhalation of the boxwoods, to pick it up again farther on, along a grassy strand. The airy message stirs his senses, points a direction— the shortest distance—and links him to the female whose broadcast scent assures him that on his ardor all her hopes are pinned. His moral mission as a freebooter is now spiced with the prospect of pleasure to be had, and the sooner the better.

Gone, the guise of the casual stroller; see in its place the impetuous lover, making his way into the garden enclosure. Over mallows and a border of thyme he soars, past pools of periwinkle and phlox. Finally, where a dense clump of rose-mary curves away, he espies the female with the erotic aroma. She is poised on the edge of a blossomy spike, sticking her abdomen out from the bright pink sepals and green petals in a posture denoting consent. The odor has suddenly acquired the shape expected, and our drone swoops down upon it without further ado. He climbs up, grips, rubs the other's flank, and plunges into the soft brown fur. So much for preliminaries: head pointing toward the center of the blossom, his huge dark eyes lost deep among the stamens, he attempts with short, jerky movements to perform the act of mating.

The performance is not working, as he rapidly becomes aware. Though taken aback, he persists, but to no avail. There is something abnormal here, something beyond his ken, per-haps even something suspect. Yet this is not his first experi-ence, and he is perfectly well up on what lovers do and how they do it. He pricks the pilosity, but there's the rub: he can-not find an orifice at the generally accepted spot. Could the girl possibly have a congenital malformation? Has her orifice yet to be pierced?

He is still trying vainly to comprehend, when he is made brutally aware of being gripped by a male of his own species, similarly attracted and highly excited by the powerful scent of the female, which accounts for the misunderstanding. In any case, spasmodic movements—not his own—leave no doubt about what the unwelcome intruder is trying to do to him. Bee number one writhes, wriggles, and struggles. The newcomer hangs on, clings tight, and derives even more stimulation from this active resistance. Not for a moment does bee number one consider taking advantage of all the confusion to experience, after a fashion, such pleasures as a female partner might feel. Moral indignation holds him back, that and an utter distaste for those same-gender relations called "mirror-image sex." He struggles even harder, with all the conviction that a mixture of anger, shame, and abhorrence can inspire in a bumblebee. At last, still firmly fixed to his female prize, he manages to shake free. The other fellow, feeling somewhat knocked around, flies away in a deep buzz of irritation, with not the remotest apprehension of what he has just been through; off he goes to seek adventure elsewhere, his undiminished ardor henceforth tinged with caution.

The first bee, finding that he is alone once more, resumes his eager courtship but is still unable to achieve climax. Gradually his desire wears thin with striving. It crosses his mind that the activity into which he is pouring so much effort will come to naught and be fruitless, and this suspicion rouses him to one final, desperate attempt.

As his amorous antics move him this way and that, he succeeds only in smearing himself more and more with pollen. Shiny yellow powder is clinging to his hairs. There is no point continuing. He sets off once again on his travels, seriously disturbed, frustrated, and still in a state of arousal. Not far away, he spots another female, and she, too, offers a hairy abdomen protruding from a spike of blossom. Surely this time he will have better luck and not end his day on a stiff and painful note of failure. He repeats the operation, takes a firm grip in mating position, and goes through the same simple, jerky, normally quite effective motions. But only to meet with the same disappointment. This new partner proves as impossible to penetrate as the first. Bewilderment increases. These rebuffs are getting harder and harder to swallow. It's as though his honor and virility were at stake: what good is a male if he cannot prove his masculinity? Meanwhile, though, as he thrashes around spasmodically, the pollen clinging to his hairs is spread over the moist stigma of the flower, and so the flower is fertilized. All this completely unbeknownst to the frantic, increasingly frustrated lover, who refuses to believe this is some sort of practical joke and courageously opts for a third try with a third flower.

In fact, he will go from one counterfeit bee to the next, wearing himself out without ever having his pleasure, and in every case the counterfeit bee is just the labellum of an orchid that has taken many millennia to perfect a strategy involving true mimetic deception.

This orchid known as the bee orchid, straight, slender, securely anchored in chalky soil, displays a few spiky blossoms at the tip of a rigid stem. Rooted, with no hope of ever being able some day to move about, its only recourse was to catch the attention of a chance visitor, to devise a trap or lure, bearing in mind that love is the most irresistible attraction of all. Over eons of time, the orchid's labellum, which does not have a spur, puffed out, swelled like a bitten lip, and evolved till today it bears an astonishing resemblance to a bee's abdomen. The flower has pushed illusion to the point of perfection by covering this shape with soft, thick, light-brown fuzz, on which may be seen a square spot of pale gold.

Wearing this disguise and makeup, the flowery impostor set out to ensnare a single visitor from the large family of hymenopterans, for she had resolved that she would appeal to none but him. Her trap—counterfeit copulation—was reserved for the bumblebee drone.

What remained was the problem of spreading by word of wind the message that she was there and available. So the bee orchid, in the secrecy of her slender laboratories, labored to distill a fragrance of ever-increasing complexity till she could successfully produce and reproduce at will the strong scent a female bee exudes when she is ready for love. The drone's reaction is one of total confusion; he responds to the strong olfactory appeal, recognizes the shape on the rim of the blossom, and receives a final stimulus, this one tactile, as he convulsively drives deep into the soft brown fur of the labellum.

In short, the bee orchid, acting with utter cynicism and cold-blooded efficiency, channels the amorous passions of the males toward a single goal: her own fertilization. Her perverse intelligence dimly grasped the fact that for the operation to succeed it was necessary, indeed absolutely essential, that the visitor be frustrated. It would not serve her purpose if the drone, his desire satisfied at the end of his endeavors, lapsed into languorous postcoital melancholy with no immediate appetite for further matings. It is imperative that he should pursue his amorous quest from labellum to labellum, carrying from one flower to another the pollinia adhering to his hairs. And that is why he must not be allowed any sexual satisfaction.

The only risk, but a major one for the flower, is that no one will make her the object of his amorous greed. A wandering drone may never happen along, or he may turn up too late. Her cousins, in the family Orchidaceae, considered how they could best preserve the full flower of their charm for as long as possible and yet stand up to every inclemency of the weather. They solved this problem by coating their smooth, delicate skin with a thin film, a springy, waterproof cuticle. But the bee orchid has neither time nor resources for any of that. She must accept the inevitable: *her* blossoms will wither quickly, and there is nothing she can do about it.

Her secret mechanisms have provided against the eventuality that she may be so neglected. Should neither bumblebee nor bumblebee drone come to be smeared with her pollen and carry it away to another flower, then the two distinct agglutinated masses of pollen, borne by the single stamen, bend and bow either in the process of wilting or nudged by a breeze that shakes the corolla. These pollinia fall unaided into the gluey hollow of the stigma. *Et voilà:* the orchid has self-pollinated.

As for why she does not naturally settle for this simple self-pollination in the first place, to answer that question you would somehow have to penetrate the remote, sometimes tortuous recesses of floral intelligence. Perhaps this splendid duplicity hides very complex workings of the female imagination, some mysterious design, or moral depravity operating at the point where two absolute imperatives meet and touch: the lover has to be lured, but equally, the lover has to be frustrated.

Inviolate Violet

❧

She's back and in first bloom, as usual rather small, with those flower eyes that are sort of blue. She's back, though winter might well return to inflict more bruises, nips, or final snowfalls.

Here and there in the garden's dreary confines, she can see primroses and grape hyacinth, who have been as eager as herself to thrust back up out of the ground, and the daffodils with their moistly luminous, yellow inflorescence. Everywhere else there is only garden rubbish, streaks of mud, acrid swirls of water in which stems have not quite finished rotting, and a sparse little jungle of abandoned, dried-up tendrils. A few birds are greedily gleaning the last of the previous year's fallen seeds. The air you breathe has a lingering desolate smell of distant death, as though from bluish plums rotting in a tub whence an alcoholic effluvium rises to be lost in the icy wind.

The violet has come early, but she wants to be sure that she can get her regular seat at the show—in the balcony formed by a stone edging—and also save places for her sisters-to-be.

Her way of settling in is tuft by tuft. Long stolons, lying flat to the ground, grow outward, mold themselves to any features of the terrain in their path, and take root to produce distinct new individuals. These shoots will go around an obstacle, take hold in front of it, or divide off in different directions. Always at risk, they move along with quiet determination, never stopping, toward some ideal destination, an unknown place that may already be occupied by an alien flower. And when the plant does come to a halt to take a firm, finely rooted foothold, no doubt it's because some subtly informed impulse is telling her to, and also because she is by temperament one part diviner, able to detect the perfect spot. A spot where so far there is no one else and where she has a chance of becoming what she is, an indiscreet discreet young female, secretly and ardently sexual.

As she extends netwise, a process that seems to go on with no help from her, the violet is exclusively concerned with producing her flowers. Each of these will bloom singly, on a stem originating directly from the root and not shared with other blossoms, while slender scapes separately bear the ribbed oval leaves.

The floral architecture here is neat, sober, attractive, and free of needless intricacies. It makes its statement mainly via the color to which the flower has given her name and the fragrance she exudes, a heady, penetrating scent, which, once inhaled, will be recognized again wherever it may be wafted. Subtle but persistent, the odor serves to convey her presence and availability. It stirs desire that is at first unfocused, just a poignant, uncertain allure until finally the color is perceived and an insect, its senses now fully aroused, is drawn irresistibly into the charmed circle.

Surely these are not flowers but eyes. Frosty, fragile flower-eyes, whose color was arrived at through a judicious mix of red and blue. It's as though her inner self held a free, passionate balance between the mind and the senses, between the tumult of love and a kind of proper reserve. Or again, as though this hue were a rather aloof statement of what has emerged after lengthy elaboration, after a private distilling process in which every conflict has been resolved and the hidden mystery of her subtle sensations has been acted out.

The eyes observe apparently unmoved; at any rate, if the images they capture do stir up emotions, the eyes give no hint of this. Could the violet be feeding her fantasies and her boldest dreams on the love scenes she spies round about her?

A golden rose beetle ends his noisy low-altitude flight by diving voluptuously into the folded petticoats of a rose. Blue argus butterflies, happening upon one another as they flutter restlessly to and fro, light upon a flower stem to couple. They turn to face away from each other, only their rear parts welding them together, their wings folded tight like two brush-strokes on the artist's canvas. A bumblebee drone forces the fragile septum of a monkshood blossom. In another corner, a swallowtail butterfly is busily sucking liquid up into a distillery splashed with yellow. Does the violet reach a point where, deep inside, she almost physically shares all this titillation she has been watching? Unless, of course, she strictly limits her indiscretion to a detailed enjoyment of the butterfly's magnificent color spectrum, that patchwork wonder with a series of blue mirrors along the edge of its wings.

Something, call it a many-voiced passion, welling up from nowhere and everywhere, burrows through bark, filters like fluid fire through fibers, and sends blood coursing more keenly through veins. Within the garden all is now vibrant, joyful, and impatient. Drunken buzzings, bees writhing in the heart of moist corollas, assignations on the wing, fever pitch on a microscopic scale. In this heightened atmosphere colors deepen and fragrances become more intoxicating. Creatures burning with desire seek their mate, give their all, drain their last drop of energy. Spasm-punctuated dances are performed upon earth's naked grain or where bodies interlaced trace shimmering characters in the air. During April and May, the garden turns into a scene of mass copulation, a den of debauchery, a ballet of lovemaking, whether swift or quite the opposite: delicate, drawn out, and subtle. There are lovings that take place in plain view, scorning to hide, and others that are clandestine, furtive, wrapped about by shadows in whose secret care the matings seem at once protected and protracted. And at nightfall pale gold messages, sent by winking lantern semaphore, signal the presence of glowworms and fireflies disposed to amorous embrace.

So the violet, looking on aristocratically, lives other people's loves. She never seems aroused, or even aware that she, too, has visitors. The result is that she neglects her own need to be fertilized. Her spring blossoms will remain sterile. It amounts to gratuitous display, allure for the sake of being alluring. The violet offers up her charms at no profit. There she is, bestowing pleasures and sensations upon her guests, but with no ulterior motive, never asking anything in return. Perhaps she is totally absorbed in witnessing the daring dance displays put on by others.

Throughout the spring, her leaves have been imperceptibly growing, broadening, and drawing closer together till now they form a canopy of green darkness, sheltered from inquisitive scrutiny. The violet shuts herself privily away. Safe from prying eyes, she turns her attention to the pleasure of a secret ritual, a refined ceremony of self-fertilization involving delicate caresses behind closed doors.

Deep in shadow, during the first days of August, a second flowering develops. This flowering is special and unusual, for its flowers never bloom: they stay curved in bud. In the cloistered dressing rooms formed by her leaves, the plant obeys an urge to turn circularly inward upon herself, to forget everything and lead a more confined life free of care. *These* flowers, it would seem, need no longer heed the laws and morality, the tumult and conflict, of an outside world that will never see them open. In strict privacy, the violet now appears to enjoy the fullness of her deepest self, starting with the miracle of feeling alive here and now. She wakens to a mysterious, exquisite, sensually disturbing existence, in which, seemingly, thoughts no sooner form than they evaporate in delicate, nervous tremolos.

Rapt in self-contemplation, she feels the stirring of her slender organs. Tiny, tentative touches are given and received, slight quiverings felt, thrusts and withdrawals as stamens move toward the moist places of stigmas. Pollination is accomplished with no outward parting of the petals. In the secrecy of the bud, in self-embrace, the violet brings about the fertile fusion of her opposing parts.

The Primrose and Her Prohibitions

*Y*outhful and modest in appearance, exuding and con-
veying an impression of virginity (by which is meant
readiness as yet untried), the primrose quietly displays
her single flowers of pale yellow. Five petals, joined, but
notched for accessibility, are almost entirely hidden in a long,
puffed, light green calyx, with a "wide-open eye" or dark yellow "star" down in the center, and orange marks leading to the
nectaries. Tucked privately away, the flower's tiny organs of
reproduction can just be discerned.

The leaves, for their part, are turned out and down against
the ground in a rosette, the way a collarette might be arranged
to enhance a charmingly revealed bosom. The leaves are shot
through with tiny swellings between the veins, and the result-
ing pattern gives a feeling of luxuriance. In fact, the plant
seems to have concentrated all her exuberance in her leaves so
that she can present her flowers as models of decorum, with
the slight suggestion of aloofness this requires, and perhaps a
hint of airy desire.

The primrose looks as though she would be carried off by the first wind that blows and would scatter in the breeze without leaving a trace; as though she has decided once and for all in favor of slimness, and so has renounced all earthly passions along with the brutality of copulation and the notion of kinship. She does not strike you as being of flesh and blood beneath that angelic frailty, so that, supposing her to have a skeleton, it would have to be built with nothing but finely stretched threads of spun glass.

And yet, couldn't this overly decorous, fragile temperament hide a certain perversity, in the form of a self-imposed ban, or an unrelenting search for purity, or some ethical code meant to improve on nature?

The primrose knows very well how attractive she is. Where other species develop complex structures and hatch clever schemes, she gets along quite nicely on her honeyed scent and her pastel shades. A shy creature? Don't be too sure. Say rather a virgin who is ready to serve but sets high moral standards. Not only has she established her rules and prohibitions, her limits not to be exceeded, but she is clever and resourceful enough to enforce them.

Visitors come flocking. The bumblebee may be seen alighting, the drone, too, butterflies of every sort, while moths are clandestinely made welcome on her night-bedewed blooms. Taking their cue from the flower's own attitude, these visitors behave with propriety and—one might say—respect, delicately deploying their labrums, their palps, or their suckers. They unroll and extend the proboscis that they use as a drinking straw. And as their proboscises are of varied lengths, they probe the flower's intimate parts to various depths.

Though at first sight all alike, primroses are in fact of two kinds. The first kind exhibits a stigma stretching up like a pin-head in the center of the calyx, with the pollen-covered stamens remaining concealed. Conversely, in the second type, a much reduced stigma has withdrawn inside the flower and what emerges farthest are the stamens. Between these two, the primrose has deliberately built a relationship based on complementarity and crossover. With these inverse organic arrangements in place, only primroses of opposite kinds contrive to fertilize one another, whereas consummation of love between flowers of the same type proves impossible or at least unproductive.

One can imagine that in the early days of her history, the primrose was forced to self-pollinate, but that such an undemanding form of intimacy soon became boringly repetitious and then repugnant, like an onanistic nasty habit, though it did, of course, ensure continuity of the species.

In our conjecture, at some point she started wishing that she could transfer pollen to fecundate a sister plant, who would be just like her and might very well return the favor. This required a romantic go-between, love's messenger, or more to the point a spore bearer. And so the primrose prepared to make herself enticing, to give off a honeysweet fragrance, to draw visitors, captivate them, and reward them for services they were unwittingly going to perform. The reception she held was perfect in every way, and numerous were the guests taking up her invitation to sample a delicately flavored cocktail. Under the gentle touch of those tiny proboscises busily probing her private parts, the flower experienced sensations such as she had never known, a tickling stimulation that was far from unpleasant. Her greatest satisfaction was a prim little feeling of vanity or vainglory at being so successfully seductive. Tremulous, she felt herself wakening to a wholly new life that could easily carry her away, out of control. The sexual fever, nay, fervor, of her visitors was contagious, rousing her to a confused kind of passion. A tide of rebellion rose in her, an ill-defined wish to break away, and even a precocious desire for innovation in response to newfound sexual promptings. But for now, the main concern was that her seed should finally be going somewhere else, outward bound toward corollas not her own. At least this would involve a relationship between self and another. There was just one problem: she and the other would be so completely identical that any sensations she sent out would almost immediately be returned for the sender to enjoy, familiar and unchanged. What was missing was the element of novelty, genuine outbreeding, an encounter with the one who is not you, who you will never be, the male or female destined to render you magically complete, all the things that make happiness three-dimensional, suspenseful, and essentially elusive.

It all began with a nameless desire spreading throughout the species, raising fears but also bursts of jubilation before there was anything to celebrate. The desire grew, becoming more intense, more and more dominant. Filling the mind, it then became an idea, increasingly obsessive. Now it was an idea-driven desire, wild, daring, sublime, possibly perilous but opening unexplored vistas, literally reinventing love as a mutual magnetic attraction with each half seeking to recover its lost unity.

By the time the idea took shape, desire had long since convinced them all, with no need for consultation. The primroses became uniformly imbued, not to say impregnated, with the idea. They thereupon divided into two tribes. On the near and farther sides of a boundary that from then on could only be crossed by delegating a messenger, they set about transforming their private selves, imperceptibly enlarging or cutting back the instruments of their sexuality to produce opposite kinds of plant. Some opted for a stiffly erect visible stamen while their stigmas withdrew into the flower. Contrariwise, the others preferred a stigma coming up to the surface while their pollen-bearing stamen retreated deep into the flower. The primroses thus made it impossible for any one of them to have fruitful relations with a sister plant of the same type; they chose sexual relations based on perfect complementarity, and differentiation based on trust and loyalty. Simply stated, they chose crossing and pairing.

What is really fascinating about living creatures, when desire arises, is the way intelligence steps forward to serve aspiration and in so doing extends the realm of the possible. It seems a constant truth that everything is simply waiting for an inspiration or inner signal, a need or intense longing. Once a basic idea has welled from the soul to permeate the fibers, everything crystallizes around the idea and helps turn it into a reality. Perhaps any desire that is strong enough can be realized, for with every desire comes the gift to make it happen.

Today, when the primrose wants to build, regenerate, adapt, or multiply, she looks away from herself toward another, while keeping intact—so far as can be judged—that virginal quality commonly ascribed to her.

Name—Hyacinth, Grape. Occupation—Vamp.

🌱

*C*ertainly this vamp is out to seduce, but her allures are her very sweet-smelling breath, used with capricious finesse, and the color of her blossoms: clustered like a minuscule bunch of grapes, they have an amethyst hue especially attractive to insects. Closer observation, however, preferably with a magnifying glass, reveals that this arrangement of floral coloring and scent is designed solely to attract and does not include any nectar or ovarian style. If you take a razor blade and make a short incision at the base of the perianth, what you can now see is that under the "grape cluster" are other blossoms. The hidden blooms are brownish and undistinguished, but they do have nectar to offer in exchange for meticulous probing of their private parts.

The flower's outer display, with its provocative color and heady perfume, seems to be the stock-in-trade of the professional teaser. When an insect responds, all he meets at first is barren rejection and blank frigidity. But if he persists and pushes on past these allurements, he will find that the grape hyacinth has not lost sight of her ultimate goal: she wants to be pollinated.

Once inside, the visitor begins to feel that the world is shrinking round him into violaceous gloom: the walls are closing in on every side, and now he fills all the space, takes up all the room there is.

The color is profoundly affecting his senses, and he scrabbles busily around, but to no avail. At first his efforts are merely routine; familiar pleasure is at hand, or so he hopes. A sort of obligation is involved, a matter of honor, a duty to be on top of every situation and operate at peak performance. He is sustained by unfailing readiness to take things as they are and score a speedy victory, proceeding with all due impatience and vigorous enjoyment. But either this flower is holding back or she has nothing to give. Gradually uneasiness and bewilderment creep over him; he even starts wondering whether he can make the slightest impression, cause so much as a tremor, or produce any result at all.

He's in another world, a place almost sealed off but still leaving him a way out. The normal rules of free trade don't apply here. Maybe there's a trick or secret code, a gimmick or clever device he hasn't spotted that would let him into the treasure chamber. He gropes all around and wears himself out butting against the wall. He has stumbled upon a floral structure the likes of which do not exist elsewhere; can its sole function be to lure and dupe unsuspecting strangers? Pride will not allow him to believe he is the victim of deception or entrapment, certainly not of a hoax or confidence trick. He can feel himself shrinking, as though to offer stupor and confusion a smaller target. All at once he is wracked with anxiety and mistrust. Shouldn't he be afraid, shouldn't he suspect the flower of laying a trap for him with the same voluptuous care she brings to the confection of her cosmetics, perfume, and suggestive curves? Or perhaps this is some sort of test to see how he handles that colorless floating void one occasionally encounters at the very core of lovemaking.

It's not as though he had never experienced a setback before. There are so many strange things he has to put up with, weird phenomena he can't understand but has to accept, ever so many signals and signs, guiding principles that go back forever and may well go on forever. That's not counting pitfalls to be avoided, schemes to be thwarted, sticky excretions to tear free of, and prison terms imposed for reasons beyond his grasp.

Apparently, however, as he sets forth on his many quests and expeditions, he's not letting misfortunes get him down. He still reacts positively to seductive charms and makes the most of them, in exchange for a few services that cost him very little. Every new corolla is the sudden embodiment of a privately cherished and regularly revisited dream, the kind of dream that sees him setting sail for unfamiliar shores or anyway for cozy boudoirs where our explorer doesn't always have the feeling that he's the first to set foot: he may find the sacks of pollen already gutted and the flasks drunk dry. In theory, he has the right to respond yea or nay to the appeal of certain odors and shapes, while some situations he is allowed to bypass entirely. But only in theory. In practice, his senses forever pander to his greed and sweep him away, so that before he knows it, he is deeply involved. There are temptations the insect cannot possibly resist.

Meanwhile, in the confining alcove of the grape hyacinth,

he keeps assuring himself that there can't be anything the matter. Like all her kind, this flower is exposed to the outer world, open to the stream of life and susceptible to changes in the wind. Surely, like all those others, she must worry that nothing may happen to her; she must live in dread that her visitors will arrive and depart leaving her unpollinated. Bringing to bear all his might as well as all his dreams, and bolstered by one last hope verging on absolute despair, the insect pushes stubbornly ahead. To persist means that he must forge on till he reaches the very heart of the hyacinth, worm his way into her most private recesses, and not be afraid of what he may find, however strange.

He digs with his feet, shoves with his forehead, edges through, finds the courage to go farther in. And perseverance pays. Under the purple-blue "grape bunch" that attracted him in the first place, he discovers unpretentious florets, of a more somber lackluster color. These he promptly pollinates, regaling himself with long draughts of nectar, and oblivious now to the distant sound of wind on the flower's outer wall.

Subject: Passionflower with Birds

❧

*A*ll the instruments of the Passion are said to have been inscribed on this flower. Displayed in the center of her broad, star-shaped blooms is a profusion of slender filaments, marked in blood red and representing the Crown of Thorns. The pistil is equipped with three sturdy stigmatas that suggest the three nails, while the stamens appear to be the five wounds. The anthers are like tiny hammers. There on its pedicel the single ovary is the sponge that was soaked in vinegar and held out on the tip of a stiff reed stalk. Lastly, all around, the pointed leaves are so many spear tips.

Acting from a natural superstitious tendency to see resemblances, coincidences, or identifying marks, people have transplanted certain obsessive motifs to rediscover them in the shapes imprinted on living creatures across the shadowy ages. Bypassing rational certainty, they have seized on the persistence of such phenomena in order to strengthen themselves in their convictions. Aside from being formalistic and orthodox, such behavior is in part irrational and visceral; it means someone is covertly carrying around a varied baggage of automatic signals, and these in turn probably hide serious doubts, pathological feelings of rebellion, at the very least unresolved fears.

However that may be, we are told of unmistakable signs to be found in nature. See how the stars, plants, and rocks yet bear the stamp of the gods! said an earlier generation. See how the bones of this frog, after we have smothered the creature and delivered it up to the ants, reveal those selfsame instruments of the Passion! said eighteenth-century sorcerers. And it all goes to prove there was a Sacrifice, stemming from original sin and redemption, and taking place amid a race of humans so corrupt that an "Immaculate Conception" was required in order for the child god to be born. What a sad worldview, imposed upon our minds and senses by the spoilers and still (even as we reject it) hampering and frustrating us when we reach out for "the pleasure to be found in life itself." Moreover, if we are supplied in advance with a quick and easy guide to recognition cum interpretation, we will be prevented in this particular instance from experiencing the reality of a flower, the deep beauty of its colors and construction.

Far from the guilt-edged love "in which somebody dies for us so that our sins may be forgiven," it behooves us to read into the passionflower a symbol of more uplifting passions. Perhaps what we ought to detect is an intimate, richly endowed emblem of the female body or its genital jewel case. But wouldn't that constitute another betrayal of the flower, burying it beneath a different projected image? Magnifying the flower on the one hand, reducing it to the bondage of faith on the other, come to the same thing when all's said. Shall we never be done with establishing symbols and looking for signs that the cosmos has taken due note? What we should really seek is access to the world of reality and the world of dreams.

The passionflower grows against walls having a southern exposure. She clings to rubblestone, gets a tight grip on the slightest irregularities, and sticks her green fingers into crevices. Hers is the existence of a climbing vine. Let her but consider how satisfied she is with her many reliable connections, and she will grow even more; she will spread out, unfold, and in the abundance of her pointed leaves, reveal attributes that strike the beholder as tropical.

Her beauty does not belie her island origins or distant lifetimes lived among parrots, shards of coral, and the odors of castor-oil plants. A Creole immigrant, you might think, still gaudily appareled, lush and vital in her changing moods, richly endowed with brilliant colors that speak out in sun and shadow, in the blues of sea and sky combined, or in old memories suspended by astrolabes and the perfect proportions of golden numbers.

So you would expect, in the luxuriance of her green underskirts and especially in among her blossoms, to breathe perfumes of spice, vanilla, sea urchin, or ripe mango, but in fact the plant gives off virtually no scent of any kind. Her fragrance is almost non-existent. Would that be the reasoned reticence of someone not wanting to be more noticeable than she already is? The prudent precaution of an immigrant woman in these unhappy times? And yet she has to attract visitors. All these wonders must not go to waste; and besides, if she is to be fecundated, the flower can't very well bring her stamens and style together by herself.

In her odorless state, she deliberately does not attract insects. Any who do happen to venture near are creatures with a highly developed sense of smell. Perhaps she finds insects too full of hustle and bustle, too metallic, and at the same time self-serving, servile, contemptible, and cold. Mechanical jointing restricts their movements. Above all, to her way of thinking they lack imagination, sensorial spontaneity, or any refined understanding of what it means to celebrate life and savor its pleasures. With that Creole temperament, the passionflower considers her attractions deserve a more stylish approach; her chosen suitors will be drawn from a different class.

From the moment her blooms appear, she is the object of a joyful siege by the birds whose watchtowers, reconnaissance positions, and surveillance posts are on the garden perimeter. In fact, with their piercing vision, they are sensitive to any stimulus caused by light, including rich combinations of colors and shapes. Of all the flowers that the garden has to offer, only Passiflora really attracts and enthralls birds. Her frank, generous allure probably makes her the flower most apt to find common ground with that full-blooded avian temperament, its flashing diamond lights and subtle moods. It's as though the birds were hovering round a tale of the islands or round a pirate's chest whence wonders are being brought out for their delight. Into this brave new world they dive, poking their beaks at the exotic array of colors. Now and again, protecting their treasure, they raise their heads and emit intimidating cries for all to hear. Soon the air is filled with quarrels, squabbles, beak-to-beak disputes, and flying feathers. The tumult of beating wings pierces straight into your breast and reverberates there, till you would swear it had replaced the steady pulsing of your heart.

The passionflower seems to enjoy this excited, greedy, cheerful activity in which she plays the dual role of cause and prize, as though such moments brought back to some small degree the exuberance of a former life. She rewards her guests with intoxicating nectar and lets them drink their fill. The nectar has collected in a cup-shaped hollow bordered by the filaments of the crown. There the liquid brilliance is well away from the ovary, which consequently comes to no harm. As he slakes his thirst, the bird sways, and in so doing carries out all unawares the act of pollination, a bringing together of stamen and style in the resplendent privacy of the flower's reproductive parts.

Journey to the Center of the Iris

❦

*T*hose irises in their serried ranks pop out all over the garden; great numbers of them wait only till February to thrust their narrow bayonet-shaped leaves up above ground. Chalky terrain suits them quite well, as do sparse, pebbly soil and glaciated stones crisscrossed with irregular hairline cracks like a three-dimensional jigsaw puzzle.

Year by year the irises enlarge their colonies and look identical in the mass, while in fact remaining distinct. Profusion as a reaffirmation of individuality, so to speak.

The flower's structural outline defies logic. It looks like a fragile, delicate, ethereal puff of smoke. Like the frozen moment of takeoff for flight, long scarves trailing. An aerial temple, with entrances so numerous that they have to be hidden. Or again, a bizarre tent-pavilion, its flaps extended with nothing holding them up. Depending on the species, the iris is colored pale blue, purple blue, white, blue with white stripes, blue with a yellowish cast, or it is even more richly decorated in slate red with veins of darkest blue. The blossom on its hollow stem suggests an accidental production at the end of a glassblower's rod.

Let us examine the blossom in greater detail. The perianth divides into three drooping sepals and three erect petals; the petals curve in upon themselves to form the standards. In the middle of the blossom is a silky reception cavity, also sumptuously ornate, and composed of three styles having double panels that conceal the stigma.

To penetrate farther into these secret places built to a scale different from ours, what we must do, circumstances permitting, is exercise the simple talent of a spiritualist medium and slip into the body of a bumblebee. We must shrink to the buzzloud volume of his wings and deftly don his furry little brown uniform. Lastly, we have to adapt our eyes to patchwork vision and check to ensure that our tiny instruments are in perfect working order, at the same time keeping our senses highly tuned and our wits sharp.

A remark in passing: have you ever noticed how people instinctively—and perhaps quite wrongly—find it easier to envisage slipping under the skin of a butterfly or the gilded carapace of a rose beetle than into the body of let's say a sperm whale or a bush elephant? Shrinking comes more naturally. Hugeness tends to make us think of bottomless pits we can never hope to fill. In the same way, for most of us the microcosm of an anthill seems closer to our reach and better scaled to our mental grasp than the macrocosm of the galaxies.

Anyway, here we are, a honeybee; leading a life probably no worse than any others, and with nothing in those others to be envied, when once you are a bee. Then let us be a bee to best advantage, taking into consideration what bees are like and what they do best.

To begin with, we're required to wander around, zigzag along, alight here or there on silken lips and check out the occasional corolla of the ordinary sort. Undulating waves of warm air alternate with zones of cooler air, or currents of frankly frigid air in the shadow of the walnut trees. At times we have the impression that everything is flickering, sliding out of sight, and that there are holes, gaps, pools of light marked Do Not Enter, though we end up crossing them just the same, flying on with calm determination. As the air moves this way or that, particles of scent are released and come our way, inviting us to track them back to their source. But when we arrive, we may find to our disappointment that someone has already raided all the stores and drunk up all the magic liquors.

The graceful pollen dances, staged farther along in the lee of the hazel trees, are best avoided. For us, the roundabout route, always the roundabout, shaded route. Always the preferred option of the curve, the longest distance between points. Other detours, too, just to keep in shape or for the sheer pleasure of flying and enjoying the view from the air. We emerge into dusty sunlight; everywhere are spangles of liquid gold. Colors call to us invitingly. All of a sudden, in the shadeless noon, a low-level reconnaissance brings into view the iris's extravagant outline. She is giving off very little scent or none at all, relying just on cinematic flash to trigger our senses.

Let us, then, eagerly alight. The eagerness is of course understandable, but we would do well to bring it under control pretty sharply if we wish truly to benefit from the present moment. Or rather, if we would be a presence in the present moment, inwardly attentive to the reasons for this silent, vast display and its secrets.

Oddly enough, at close range the colors and bright patches are not mutually reinforced but instead imperceptibly neutralize one another and are reduced to a luminous maze in which shapes, it seems, all melt into a blur. Only the veins of the sepals stand out clearly, continuing to mark the path that will lead us to the nectaries.

First we reach an apse where banners stand unfurled; then, venturing farther, an alcove whose nature we cannot fathom, noiseless and unshadowed. And if noiseless, what is the source of this deafening echo? It dawns on us and soon we are convinced, that in this place life ceases to be life, becoming something more but something never named. Our breathing slows; the throbbing of our pulse is barely discernible. We are apart from the world, isolated in some private room. A light is glimmering, but we can't tell where it's coming from. We're a thousand leagues from anywhere and yet so near, pressed against a satin membrane with, so we suspect, nothing on the other side, just a colorless void.

The universe has almost shut its door upon us, and we know a deep strange sense of peace, peace that passeth all understanding. We experience a dilation of the pores, and at the same time a sort of self-abandonment, as though without quite realizing it we were about to let go of our being and delightfully dissolve. Nothing matters any more, least of all a return to the bustling hum and routine looting of the outside world. Why bother going any farther or turning elsewhere in our quest for pleasure and profit when the triumphal conclusion to the race we have run is right here? This flower has invited us to a private reception and in greatest secrecy is making every effort to serve us her intoxicating liquors.

During the aperitif, we seem to sense—but this is by the way and scarcely noticeable—a kind of tensing in the fibers of the blossom, rather like a slight circular contraction in her fine texture.

Might she not be keeping close watch on herself, alert to the least quiver in her flesh? Her invisible eyes are no doubt spying from every quarter on this trespasser (for that's what we are), but she is not giving herself away, not allowing a hint of emotion to show through, nor letting so much as a tremor escape her. She acts as though her pleasure derived exclusively from the few moments of light physical contact our movements occasion: the tickling from our legs or the probing of our little, prying proboscis.

But while we are guzzling ourselves into oblivion, the iris on the contrary is gradually regaining possession of her wits, till finally she interrupts the pleasurable shiver that was reaching down into her sensitive flesh. It is simply unacceptable that a moment of euphoria should make her forget why she is holding this reception. In a swift turnabout, the flower activates a stamen concealed just above the heedless nectar-swilling bee and starts generously coating her visitor's back with pollen. At last the bee has finished sucking the magic liquor. Impelled by the hope of fresh rewards, he takes wing, bound for the next iris blossom. There, deep inside the silken alcove, a shining stigma literally sweeps him free of the pollen he is carrying. And fertilization has occurred.

Of Other Intimate Visits

And who shall blame us for our pang of envy when we watch the bumblebee, newly lit upon a poppy, unhesitatingly shove his way into her crumpled pink underskirts? In the course of his carefree aerial promenade, chance has set temptation in his path; and once the bee's attention has been caught by the color and that adorable rumpled effect, the lush invitation is irresistible. He finds his way in among the panels and scrabbles busily till he is swallowed up.

Before we proceed, let us take a moment to observe how the poppy, acting in considerable haste, achieves that petticoat look. First a green sheath appears, already swollen and covered with long, clearly separated hairs. The sheath splits, and its segments part, yielding to pressure from the corolla seeking to unfold. All this happens in a great hurry, as though a many-faceted joy, too long suppressed, had now burst forth. No fuss or fanfare, but the jubilation does want to find full expression in a combination of strength, sophistication, and fragility. Perched on the blossom sits a kind of hat; already withered, it now comes loose and the corolla puffs up again, unrolls, smooths its wrinkles, and stretches out in close ranks of petals like the pink swish-swish of a ballerina. Surely this undergarment was confined for too long in a chrysalis, existing almost inanimately; otherwise how could it blossom out completely in no time at all? The poppy takes her frothy rustling allurements of palest red and waves them in the sun. At the most intimate place in the flower, a corona of pollen-powdered stamens surrounds milady ovary. She, sporting a bonnet with velvet bands, waits for visitors to come, bringing her a coat of fecundating dust.

The moment he disappears among the petticoats, our bumblebee appears to be pulled in as though by suction. An observer might well wish to experience that sort of immersion for himself; as it is, he can only look on, with envious fascination. Wouldn't it be nice, we find ourselves thinking, just to slip into that corseted little body, take part in its movements and share the excitement. In fact, this imagined approach is the only way we have of becoming physically (so to speak) involved.

We enter a wonderfully rumpled, hermetic world that whispers as we draw near. This domain is an exquisite, tight-packed mystery that we do not comprehend, nor seek to comprehend, though we certainly trust to benefit from it by working our way into the flowery folds. A few silken utterances are lost in the intricacies of the flower, and just as well: there is no point expounding enigmas when we are absorbed in sensual pleasure. In fact, it works the other way; the enigma enhances our savoring of pleasure, adding a slight, tantalizing, metaphysical dimension that we rather like.

On the other hand, something that would be welcome is a bit of oily moisture oozing out of nowhere or everywhere to make our descent smoother; but, oh, well, the smoothness of the petticoats will do. Down and in we go, quite comfortably, with petals brushing against us from all sides—a novel sensation. Our wings are pressed close to our body. Objects are indistinguishable as we move along. This is the path a bee must take, the highroad to high delight.

Not for one moment does the bumblebee imagine that the flower is giving in to him without reserve, and so he sets out to discover what more she might have to offer. What he finds are slender sacs of pollen and a trickle of ambrosia that wells up to meet him under the pressure of his legs. Stubborn persistence has found its reward. In the roseate semidarkness of the poppy, the bee's tongue seems to punctuate a great adventure-filled dream.

By and by the rumpled petals begin to heave silently, with spasms of shaking. These are the first signs that the insect is about to resurface. Then the petticoats gape open, smoothen a bit, and allow the bee to emerge, drunken and groggy. He pulls himself together, not bothering to wipe off a powdery pinkish bloom he has acquired, and still nursing an undefined, lingering dream. Perhaps he ought to consider that the details of the dream, and its sequence of events, are worth remembering.

*   *   *

For purposes of floral visitations, the bumblebee is provided with a rigid tongue or proboscis. More precisely, the labium is more elongated than the labrum and forms a flattened tongue with hairs all along it and a central groove that enables it to suck up nectar. As the body is stiff and furry, grains of pollen readily adhere, sticking to the head, the corselet, and especially the sturdy, flexible currycomb carried on the abdomen. Pollen is conducted to the leg-joint articles, where it is gathered and then stocked in long pouches housed in the thickness of the thigh. As described, the bee's entire body is a formidable little harvesting machine.

Depending where his aberrant wanderings take him, and always on his own initiative, he may find his way into a simple, undemanding petal arrangement or into more complex structures, corollas where colored shadow unfolds its mysteries and bestows its favors. Every incursion is an adventure, leading by progressive stages into the private life of a flower. On each occasion, the bee will suddenly be immersed in a very special atmosphere, consisting this time of insignificant bits and pieces, next time of formal inner sancta lined with satin, silk, and precious stuffs. These more elaborate interiors will have special markings, spots or reddish signposts to captivate the insect and lead him enthralled to the private apartments.

Sometimes he behaves expertly, skillfully, with astonishing intelligence; on other occasions he is anxious, overeager, fumbling and tumbling all over himself in his rush to get drunk on those liquors down inside. There may be some fearful secret that the flower hasn't confided to him, some snare set beneath the petals. He subjects the whole situation to careful scrutiny, probably adding a dash of caution, but that heady perfume, broadcast by the plant like an advertisement, gets the better of him. This is the ad that keeps its promise, the offer you can't resist. When that happens, something is added to the routine of ordinary pleasures: sensual delights of a more serious nature, distinct from all those others. He is subjugated by sensations he had not imagined, hitting him at point-blank range, just when his perceptions are a bit muddled by the silken rustling of a corolla. The flower seems to quiver as he moves along; he is much gratified at producing such an effect and takes this for a sign of encouragement, an invitation to delve deeper.

In his younger days, the bumblebee may see more devilry or more magic than reality when contemplating the organs of a flower. But he very soon becomes emboldened, accustomed, relatively inured to surprises. He learns to spot similarities of signposting or layout and makes straight for the treasured object of his lust. He rolls twisting and turning in the hollow of a corolla, unwittingly bending the stamens toward the moist brilliance of the stigmas.

Actually, all this is slowly shifting and modulating in wondrous silence, where uncertain, barely perceptible undulations rock slender shadows to and fro in the floral alcove. And there, suddenly, is a mysterious alien presence, secret breathing, and once in a while a trap or splendid disguise. When you are a fly, or honeybee, or bumblebee, most likely you don't have a pessimistic or optimistic outlook, which largely explains how with each new flower you can enter a cheerful, enlivening, enchanted little universe.

Take for instance the world of the sage plant. Her main strategy for attracting insects lies in her purplish blue flowers, showing up against the little forest of grayish leaves that have come through the winter.

Each sage bloom opens and presents two clearly defined lips. The lower offers a convenient landing ledge. The other, swollen and colored the deep hue I spoke of, is there to catch the eye of any vagabond honeybee or bumblebee that may come tracing its crazy, carefree course through the air. The happy wanderer is always ready to tackle a job of intimate exploration.

Subtly constructed, the stamens of the sage flower have a highly perfected oscillatory mechanism. Dangling pendulum fashion from each bloom are two stamens, one longer and laden with pollen, the other shorter and bare of pollen. After the temperamentally impatient bumblebee has alighted and found his way in, he becomes intoxicated by the color and has his appetite further whetted by the discreet yet penetrating fragrance. He discovers a recessed space bathed in violet shadow and with his stiff, fuzzy body takes its measure. Once again, what was a vision seems to have acquired reality and depth. He applies himself to his usual thievery and in the process sets the pendulum moving. His hairs at once receive a charge of pollen that he will transfer—randomly and unknowingly in the course of his other calls—onto the shining secretion of a stigma.

*   *   *

Inside the private space of the lady's-slipper, an ordeal awaits us: sudden imprisonment, solitary confinement, which in our first moment of panic we might mistake for a life sentence. Always growing singly, these flowers arrange their trap with an admirably alluring color combination: the elongated sepals are red brown; the very large, swollen labellum is a ripe yellow color and hollowed out into the shape of a slender, delicate slipper marked on the inside with tongues of purple.

Our bold questing has led us into an imagined scene of Eastern splendor. Around and above us is a roughly spherical inflated tent in which a silent Oriental tale, befitting the ambient color, is opening the pages of its spells, intrigues, and wondrous dramas. Silky rustling accompanies our progress. Enchanted, we decide to allow ourselves an interval of happy self-abandon, of voluptuous ease within an expanded existence, taking our time as we aspirate the precious liquor and plunder the tiny sacs of pollen.

Around us is a space at once grandiose and confined, made larger by luxurious silence in which flashes of bright light almost create the effect of walking on a laquered surface. The setting puts us on our best behavior, inspires us to strive for fine manners, for the sort of deftness that conveys elegance of mind, even if our morphology does dispose us rather to bashing obtusely and clumsily onward.

Just for a second we have the impression that there may be someone lurking behind the draperies, spying on us. This is followed immediately, in our hymenopteran consciousness, by a dawning dream of empty space, awareness of absence or of something (for reasons delectable) prohibited. Before we realize what is happening, the slipper-shaped labellum has given way under our weight and has closed on us from behind.

We are now a prisoner. When we have grasped that fact, we somewhat scornfully assume that the problem is a mechanical failure, or a trap not meant for us, or a prank in the worst possible taste. We try shifting into reverse, then we try to disengage. The smooth inner wall baffles retreat. We slip and slide. There is not the minutest hump or bump to get a grip on. It seems to us that what we are up against here is deliberate, plotted intent, Machiavellian machination, for a purpose that is beyond our grasp and will forever elude our understanding. In the grip of mortal terror, we lose all our self-possession and thrash wildly about. Then calm returns; we go back to work, shove with our forehead and brace ourselves with our legs. These feverish efforts have no effect on the flower. Must we resign ourselves to captivity?

Even in a luxury jail featuring every modern sensual convenience, the part of a prisoner is not just to go on accepting life as "a brutish approximation." Soon the only course left open is to concentrate on his own inner resources and there to break new ground. If he wants to go through walls, he will have to give free rein to his dreams, set up a creative workshop in his skull, and develop a sense of game playing. But only under the duress of physical confinement, only when he is driven back more and more onto his own unsuspected reserves, can this superior escape mechanism be summoned up at will.

Suddenly, in the depths of our despair, when we have given up all hope of salvation, the outline of something resembling escape flashes briefly across our vision. To be precise, our legs, scrabbling at the draperies in a last-ditch effort, find a rent in the fabric. The fluid, golden light of day is ours to see again, the buzzing of other creatures ours to hear, and all the sounds of life, which has not stopped during our captivity. Through the rift we go, and hastily make good our escape, without giving way to surprise or gratitude.

The trial we have endured was cleverly devised by the flower for her own ends: as the visitor passes through the tiny split concealed in her wall, pollen adheres to his coat, and when he leaves he takes it along.

*   *   *

Atop her standards of dark green leaves, the monkshood displays her blossoms, which take their color from the purplish blue of the upper petals. On closer observation, however, the blossoms are seen to be almost shut, so that the bumblebee is obliged to exert pressure if he wants an opening. It's like having to force a safety vault whose structure is not just secure but also elegant and refined.

The bee has in his favor a sturdy, well-built physique, solid shoulders, and a broad, stubborn forehead. You wonder if he's harboring a memory, which time has not assuaged, of some humiliating experience or frustrated desire. But he puts it all behind him, determined to approach his task single-mindedly. When a flower resists the way this one is doing, that's something the bee is prepared to deal with, and he simply becomes more tenacious. He's not afraid to work up a sweat. This affrighted-maiden act, this prudery and hanging back, gets on his nerves and makes him that much more obstinate.

He works his way in until he is under the billowing tent-canvas, where everything seems to have been laid out for a ceremony or a point-by-point debate; but the bee is not about to waste time and effort in discussion or ritual. As he comes by, the stamens jab pollen into his hairs as though they were planting banderillas. He, meanwhile, goes into raptures at the sight of a fine, full set of naked organs and seeks instant intoxication in their nectar, aided by a wee but willing proboscis.

The Arum's Masterly Strategy

*astertide is when you may expect to see the arum lily. How much secret labor and ruthless scheming, there beneath the black garden humus, have gone into perfecting this beautiful, strange horned flower!

Within the circumscription of the roots, a treacherous, crafty spirit—probably no more than the removed portion of instinct—has conceived and drafted its plans, corrected problems as they came up, built and tested its shapes and private workings. Lastly, the spirit added colors it considered suitable. What emerged was a perfected floral prototype, astounding in its architectural daring. But built into this thoroughly modernist structure is a tiered and terrible trap.

The floral apparatus consists firstly of the spathe, a broad greenish-white bract, rolled to form a cone. Inside the spathe is the spadix, a violet-hued, dark velvet stalk with an enlarged head, looking like a tiny club or bludgeon. The bloom distills and emits atoms of perfume, entrusting them to the vagaries of the wind. The odors can in some cases be frankly fecal or morbid in character and are meant to attract dung-eating and carrion-eating insects. For the fastidious reader, the insects are coprophagous and necrophagous, respectively. These airborne advertisements draw the desired visitors, tantalizing them and sharpening their gluttonous appetite. They track the smells back to their point of emanation, where they discover the powerful, attractive spathe, its hollow standard jutting upward in pure avant-garde lines.

A fly has just ventured inside the vertical duct; let's follow her in her travels and tribulations.

To begin with she is unable to alight on the spathe, which is extremely smooth, offering not the slightest rough spot she can cling to. She flutters frantically down into the narrow abyss, trying repeatedly to land. The moment she comes to rest, she slides right to the bottom, onto a collarette of long, downward-folding hairs. Recovering her wits, she at once clears herself a passage into this crown of fine filaments, pedaling with her legs while burying her head farther and farther in.

Not for a moment does it cross her mind to turn back and escape by flying straight upward, so bewitched is she—and curious, too, about the arrangements made for her on the far side. The prevailing temperature in the tube is not what she is used to and she finds it rather pleasant, so pleasant indeed that she fails to notice how the hairs have closed behind her at the place where there is a constriction in the spathe.

The fly is conducted into the structure's main section, where she marvels at a glaucous light suffusing the recessed area. The warmth here becomes more pronounced and starts to make her limbs feel heavy. It's like another time and another world. In this private, silent space, she discovers a treasure-house of secreted substances and begins avidly feeding on them. At intervals she allows herself a brief pause, perhaps because it occurs to her that if she emptied all the flasks at one go, she would miss half the pleasure. Then she goes back to siphoning liqueur. Temerity has been well rewarded . . . until, having drunk her fill and now wishing to get out, she finds she is a prisoner.

For the first time, she uses her protuberant, faceted eyes to take a careful look at her sealed-off surroundings. She goes over to the wall, gropes around, tests its smoothness with the tips of her legs, and seems to detect activity: something keeps receding as she moves. It's just her own reflection, elusive and approximate, a few scarifying lineaments that it's amusing to play tag with for a moment. But she has enough problems already; it would not be a good idea to add to them by becoming the prisoner of her own image or of some phantom figure that instantly mimics her every move. Now seriously and rightly distressed, she comes away from the wall, back to the flasks that she has emptied. Her self-respect still rejects the notion that such a splendid welcome could be the prelude to a trap. Confused and helpless, she gazes up at the place where the filaments have shifted to bar the path. Then she decides that viewing the problem from a distance is inadequate, so she goes over for a closer look.

Along the spadix is a globular ring or annulus composed of male flowers. At the very bottom is another equally globular annulus, bearing a greater number of female flowers. A magnifying glass reveals that in neither gender group do the flowers have a perianth; they have reproductive organs and that's all. Each male flower displays four quite distinct stamens, while the female flowers, in the absence of both calyx and corolla, are resplendently naked with a myriad glittering dots of light. As the insect crawls over the male flowers, she picks up pollen in her hairs, then comes and deposits it on the moist stigmas of the females. Though she may not know it, her initial exploring and later her search for a way out have ensured fertilization.

Using a razor blade, I later freed that particular fly, the one we accompanied till the time of her detention and despair. I found her bewildered in her cell, taken unawares in the midst of her bustling activity and sensuous cravings. Immured with her was a colleague who had been there longer than herself. Perhaps the two of them had held private consultations on all sorts of matters, with incomprehension, frustration, and mutual compassion figuring prominently.

However that may be, when they caught sight of the unexpected breach I had opened, they sat there for a moment, dazzled by the sudden return of daylight; then they both took joyful wing, flying right past my face. But of course visitors, whether dipteran or coleopteran, do not normally enjoy the benefits of outside intervention. They have to come to terms with their captivity and fill in the time freely consuming the abundant supply of secretions. There is a certain amount of risk attached to this waiting period: the flowers can have fits of generosity that send a wave of liquid surging into the chamber, and the cloistered occupants who earlier had been feeding on the liqueur are now drowning in it. They die a horrible death, unable to ingest all they are offered, the demands of their appetite incommensurate with the overwhelming supply.

If we ignore these few extreme cases of secretionary over-flow, the arum has in fact made provision for setting her visitors free after they have performed certain services. Maturity occurs in the male flowers somewhat later than in the females; the males then expand, have a second growth and demolish the collarette of hairs located at the constriction in the tube. The prisoners are free. Away they fly, their bodies speckled with pollen.

Sometimes the spathe has to become etiolated before they can be released completely. The cone withers, rots, hangs down, and tears apart like the canvas of a comparably shaped tent. There can be no doubt that a few visitors are left pinned beneath the wreckage and suffocate. But these nameless, insignificant deaths don't matter when seen from the standpoint of the arum; *she* can only rejoice in the success of her strategy for getting fertilized.

In the first days of summer, spikes of shiny arum berries stand erect, their orange red apparently glowing from a dull internal light. They are the poisonous fruit that Jean de Bosschère described as "a fire-reddened wrought iron club."

Vagabond Queen

✤

*F*rom every side, these teeming, sorry-looking, mis-shapen hordes pour into the garden. Marauding bands of ne'er-do-wells lay siege to the cultivated space, close in on it, invade it, plunder it, and do their best to smother it in a sneaking, tenacious, parasitic embrace.

The flowers of this ragged, roving rabble are poor specimens with sickly colors. Woody stalks or tendriled creepers. Tart, floury-tasting, lumpy berries, prematurely dried-out. To our senses and our sense of self-respect, weeds bring an impression at once appalling and alarming: unbearable awareness of an existence that is vain and empty, free but to no purpose, a life fallen into decay or somehow discredited.

Yet the harder you try to eradicate them, the bitterer their determination to come right back up, grow . . . like a weed, be thoroughly untidy, and spread all over the place with no consideration for others. They are difficult to keep in check, reappear where you have pulled them out, multiply, discharge their seeds over a wider and wider area, fill out with thick, tough fiber, swarm, climb, creep, box in, encircle, gnaw, and ramify underground into a hopelessly tangled network of roots. They engage in guerilla warfare, constantly harassing.

Incidentally, I knew at first hand the case of a mother who sent her daughter out to weed the garden whenever bad thoughts took root in the child's mind. A simple form of exorcism, or quick, practical therapy, as though by mimesis this punishment would produce the same result in the girl's head as in the vegetable patch. And it so happens that on each occasion the prescribed treatment turned out to be quite effective: the girl would come in from the garden docile and conciliatory, her serenity and peace of mind apparently restored. But she also struck me as being diminished, dangerously dispossessed, as if in performing her task she had broken completely clear of a lush, dark, frivolous backdrop that in all probability was essential to her full flowering.

Noxious plants, noxious thoughts: they wreak havoc in the dark; they seem perilously, insidiously sterile. By that I mean: unbecoming, undesirable, subversive, in conflict with the established order and officially sanctioned culture. They come of bad seed and can only lead to the fringes—the fringes of cultivated gardens and cultivated society. And yet, considering society itself has reached a dead end, existence is at low ebb, and we live in stagnant times, shouldn't we consider taking a second look at all those "harmful weeds" and "harmful thoughts"? Why not turn our steps toward the fringes, the places that haven't been overtaken and denatured by cultivation? Why not venture out into the bush, the wasteland, the hollow ground, the desert islet, the neglected garden? Why not go back to the fountainhead we have walled up and proscribed, the wellspring we have banished and excluded?

In the midst of couch grass, sorrel, groundsel, madder, thistles, and tendriled vetches, the euphorbia is looked on as the heathen queen. She grows surrounded by a cursed and scattered tribe, who are forbidden to drop anchor. The devil's milk, so they say, burns in her stem, and her blue-green velvety leaves make cats go blind. One positive virtue only is she allowed: her root can ward off attacks of spleen; so people often keep one stalk of spurge euphorbia in their garden.

When you are queen of something or someplace, you can have caprices befitting your rank, freedom to follow your burning desires, and renown of the kind that attends every unpredictably stirred-up passion anywhere in the world. In matters of the heart, people expect a queen to exhibit rebellious, unbridled emotion and secret, inventive, unconquerable ardor. If need arise, they expect her to have recourse to medicines, magic potions, and other cunning devices. It's hard not to be a trifle disappointed when you discover that the euphorbia's sexual behavior is rather conventional despite the originality she displays in attracting lovers.

What flowers can possibly have put out these big warty berries, "trigons that look like unripe capers," some of them striated, and covered with tiny semispherical bumps?

It depends who's telling it. The structure of the blossom is strange. It is captivating insofar as it stands stripped bare, and the naked smoothness is further emphasized by a color not often encountered, wavering between yellowish green and gray gold. Prying the bloom partway open with the tip of a fingernail, you have a strong sense that here is either the sacrilegious or the sacred. Surely the flower's nudity expresses a long-forgotten, precious truth, the last remaining extension of an invisible line connecting her with the mysteries of her nomadic origins.

But—and this is where originality comes in—what you assume at first glance to be the bloom, broadening out as the plant blossoms, is in fact just a grouping of the flowers, a contracted inflorescence. The queen holds her audiences under a billowing canopy having hues as of pale moon. The scene is an enchanting trompe l'oeil or a box-in-a-box illusion. The visitor cannot see anything or anyone checking admission, so eventually, with a last cautious look round, and his pulse rate up a bit, he makes up his mind to go in. He finds that he has entered a circus tent or a mysterious alcove, where all is silent, empty, and bathed in a golden green light. He thinks he must have come early or else very late, before or after a show that included magicians and tightrope walkers.

Were swallow dives performed, or will they be performed later, here under the big top? Without lingering in the stands, he starts moving around out in the ring, in reality a greenish vase where there are small three-styled female blooms and single-stamened male blooms. This is all familiar stuff such as he customarily encounters whenever he commits a break-in, and he's not terribly interested (it belongs to a separate world and sexual patterns outside his scope).

What does catch his interest, on the other hand, are yellow gray oval- or crescent-shaped glands located along the sides of the tent. He immediately goes to work on them, using his legs and proboscis. Under his ardent caresses, a sugary fluid very soon comes oozing out more and more freely. He drinks the intoxicating brew till he can drink no more, leaving Queen Euphorbia to feel quietly pleased with herself for being fecundated in her royal chambers.

A Flower-carpeted Womb

*W*ith her colonies of flowers that not only are very tiny but also have no corollas, the fig tree is ill equipped to rival the grand floral attractions laid out at her feet.

Moreover, her blossoms, which rank among the smallest to be found anywhere, shut themselves away in a sort of urn, which effectively rules out the possibility that they will attract anything. The urns look rather funereal but do keep the flowers safe from harm or from the consequences of their own foolishness. Brimful of shadow, these little amphoras with their rounded sides are lost under a circularly arranged avalanche of big, thick, opaque, heavily veined leaves, slightly rough but velvety to the touch, and covered with fine hairs.

Let us take a razor edge and cut a little ways into one of these amphoras, learnedly called *syconia* by the scientists. The first thing we note is an opening (the *ostiole*) at the opposite end of the stem. This fleshy receptacle, though it is walled round like a cloister, has not shut the world out completely; it has kept a visitors' access corridor, like a narrow respiratory tract.

On the inside, the chamber is lined with flowers, male and female. The male flowers display three stamens. The female flowers are endowed with an ovary topped by a style of one or other size: some are short, some long. Even partly exposed—and remember that ordinarily it is plunged in total darkness—the cavity seems to preserve intact the mysterious privacy underlying its laws and its relationships within the community of flowers.

As will be shown, the fig we eat is simply a progressive pulpy modification in the inflorescence of the original urn. The real fruit consists of those pips that crunch against our teeth at autumn fig-tasting time. For every pip, a flower has been fertilized, an enormous output of fruit when you consider the lilliputian proportions of the flowers. The ridged lines it develops on its body delineate the fig's perfect shape, which at first glance suggests a testicle. But under more attentive scrutiny it is revealed as a symbol of intricate, concealed femininity. Moist warmth radiates toward the center, which is always hollow. A magnifying lens discloses a mix of pink and pale red, like a geode with its coralloid cohorts, a fibrous, close-packed, teeming multitude. The component parts of the flesh, laden with bright pips, seem to merge vibrantly one into the other.

But let us return to the urn-shaped inflorescence, the not quite cloistered, extremely select vase where silent loving and silent dying go on unwitnessed.

Doomed to a reclusive life, powerless to reach out and fertilize one another, the flowers of the fig tree distill a rare and subtle perfume. The scent goes forth via the communicating orifice, carrying with it all their hopes. Committed to the whims of the wind, dissipating as it wafts along, the fragrant message is designed to attract, irresistibly and imperatively, a microscopic insect. This member of the order Hymenoptera has been assigned the rather barbaric or Belphegoric name *Blastophaga*.

When the airborne perfume and its invitation suddenly hit these *Blasto* . . . perhaps we should settle for fig wasps, their senses are roused to such a fever pitch that they can't help but respond. Acting quickly, they trace the scent back to its source, reach the fig tree, flutter among the thick leaves, pinpoint the amphora-shaped growths, circle one of them, speedily locate the ostiole, and make their way into the wonderfully populous night of the syconium.

What greets the visitors' senses is a full-fledged secret harem: flowers, roped off into a balcony and all facing the moist, hollow center. Without understanding how it happened, in the course of a private break-in where a passage door was left open, they have stumbled onto a dream. They emerge from the passage into a remote Aladdin's cavern that no one knew existed, where tiny, slender creatures, packed close together like brilliants on a diadem, endlessly dispense their heady perfume, further bemusing the ardently desired intruders.

Sometimes the visitors' duct is so narrow that the *Blastophagas'* wings are broken. But wings are of no further use in the task that now lies ahead: a series of maneuvers that will mutually benefit them and the flowers in their respective love dealings.

Losing no time, they sink their ovipositors into the flowers' private parts. The short-styled blooms allow them to reach the ovary and bury their eggs in it. The long style of the other blooms prevents this, keeping the fig wasps at a respectful distance, as though the blossoms were withholding their favors to follow a special plan, a different, carefully considered, personal goal.

This means that part of the flower population is sacrificed in favor of the insects, who use those ovaries to hatch their eggs. But fair exchange is no robbery. The remaining flowers, the ones with long styles, will be fertilized by the insects: in the course of their activities, the fig wasps transfer pollen onto the delicately viscous floral stigmas. After this intense, hectic moment of sexual existence, the fig wasps expire in the warm, scented night of the syconium, leaving behind minuscule corpses that soon crumble to nothing at all, a fine, grayish dust that the community of flowers quickly absorbs into its fibers.

Later, when the insects are already dead, their offspring will hatch, in two stages. The males break their eggs first. In the larval state, they have turned the flowers' ovaries into an incubator for their own growth and development. Now, having rapidly matured, and driven by some obscure instinct that allows no time for reflection or naive wonderment, they set out for the nearby blossoms whose private organs house their sister fig wasps. The female insects are still half asleep, their senses are still dormant, but without so much as a how-d'ye-do, not even letting them come out of the flowers, the males fertilize each and every one in a spasmodic little dance.

As soon as they have performed these speedy, anonymous matings, the breathless, exhausted males in turn expire by the hundreds, there in the warm, damp, close-pressed shadows. They certainly are not aware of fate's uncertain chances, nor have they any perception of the very slender membrane that separates love and death when you are transmitting life.

While the males are gasping their last in the chambered

darkness, the unwed mothers, endowed with transparent wings, are emerging from inside the flowers. They have had no adolescence; they have been taken unawares, robbed of a natural desire that never had a chance to crystallize but instead was immediately fulfilled. Perhaps they might have wished for slow, pleasurable preliminaries, a few caresses, a romance, an initiation into love; perhaps they would have liked time to contrive an elaborate feminine allurement and put it to the test. Instead, they come fully alive only to find themselves already pregnant. But they are not about to sit there being disconsolate and irresolute amid demolished ovaries and moribund males.

Their surroundings have become futile, oppressive, and unbearable. The thing to do now is go, leaving behind their sorrows and the desires they never knew. From every quarter they converge on the single exit corridor. Crawling out into the open air, they fly straight and free toward the amphora of another blossom. And that very brief journey is the only time they will ever have savored the light of day. Already they are crawling along another ostiole, returning to the familiar darkness and moist warmth surrounding another community of flowers. Even as we speak, they have begun anew to jab their ovipositors into every available ovary.

And what of the long-styled blooms, the ones whose ovaries the *Blastophagas* couldn't reach in their generative frenzy but who instead were fertilized by having pollen brought to them? They have embarked upon the deep, slow, complicated process that sees a flower transformed into fruit. Here hangs the fig in its fleshy garment, wrapped round its reddish, moist, dark center, guarding as though in remembrance the shining relics of what were once its blossoms.

PART

II

Shrill Song from a Mixed Choir

❧

I t has to be oven hot. The light has to be almost molten, pouring strands of fluid gold through the branches. The sky turns to mineral blue; the air lies heavy over its deposits of dust. Nothing is stirring. Thick shadows. Oppression. The grass dries and yellows on its stalks. No wind.

When Sirius the Dog Star rises and sets with the sun (roughly from mid-July to mid-August), the many-voiced clamor of the cicadas is at its height. They arrange their musical composition in unvarying stanzas that always end abruptly, and their song mingles with hollow echoes, cymbals, and the clicking sound of crickets. They perform their arias, chirring with a rapid vibration of the abdomen. On every side, to the mellowing of summer they add the deafening din that was lacking.

As June ends, the cicada larvae come out of the ground and seek the slender shadows of light for their mutation. Imagine many flowers blossoming at once. Each cicada comes up from a kind of alveolus, a tomb no bigger than your thumb, but in which she was very much alive, very busy over a long period. She dug galleries toward nearby roots: away from the eyes of the world, she would drive her sucker in and get quietly inebriated on the sap retained by the plant.

She also used this vault and its corridors as a place for meditation, rest, and reflection. There, while she took shape according to a model and pattern imprinted within her, the larva was perhaps harnessing a wild dream, readying herself for promised glory, envisioning the joys and possibilities of unfettered freedom. The drudgery of burrowing was rendered less painful by the knowledge that a sustained desire (or persistent instinct) is a promise made to us by our future. If our expectations, appeals, and deep aspirations are of sufficient quality, the world never fails to respond.

The larvae already have the big black shining eyes of the cicadas they will soon be. Eyes of deep, black, diamond night, which alone can be born of earth's early memories. The stiff wings pressed against their sides, though thick and firm to withstand the roughness of the ground, already display the finely ribbed transparency of cicada wings. The entire elongated body, inured to the bustling harshness of time spent underground, has a sturdy constitution, but its pale green color, with whitish streaks, gives the creature a sickly appearance.

When they come out by boring through their covering of earth, the transition from one world to another seems to take place without a hitch, as though the endeavor involved no real border crossing. They emerge from pre-existence eager for life, drawn into the promised light. They have dreamed so many dreams about the light, mentally rehearsed the same ideas so often and put so much unfathomable conviction into the difficult task of obtaining food, all in preparation for this moment. They do not appear surprised at the wide open spaces that finally greet their eyes; they are better employed in rejoicing at the intense summer heat that will give them color and complete their limbering up.

They climb at once into the nearest bush, cling on—in fact get a viselike grip—and using their legs and clavicles, promptly work free of a long, brittle overcoat. This castoff of thin, tattered skin will hang there awhile, until the wind tears it apart or the rains dissolve it, or a bird makes off with it in his beak, thinking it has the right consistency to be some new kind of prey. At the same time, the cicadas evince not the slightest desire to look back, as though they were stepping out of an earlier role, breaking with shadowy memories, with old truths and constraints that don't apply in this new situation. The metamorphosis is complete, and the cicadas are free to fly where they will. They now resemble long, finely crafted, mysterious jewels of lovely, lustrous brown, so captivating they make you think of amulets.

Broadcasting invisibly from every corner, they instantly imprint upon the airwaves a dense orchestral arrangement of their high-decibel hymn to life. Who is this song intended for? What is meant by this penetrating, deafening instrumental performance? Their cries are not threats. Nor are they an insistent call for a partner, an amorous aria signaling, "I'm here and I'm in the mood"; no need, since the cicadas have been mingling, male on this branch, female on that, girl and guy driving their suckers into the bark side by side, right from the beginning. Could they not socialize and find enjoyment otherwise than in their own invasive noise, crackling across the kingdom of summer?

For my part, I *like* this sonorous hallelujah, which may have no meaning beyond itself. Does everything have to have a purpose and an explanation? Why should Nature not enjoy doing things for their own sake, or have bursts of aestheticism, disinterested expenditures on music, color, and ritual? In any case, summers in the South would be sterile affairs if not for the cicadas. Their churring seems to reflect archaic rhythms as well as modern influence: the *strophes* of its Grecian ode express an ultimate maturation and its *epodes* a fullness.

Around the plant stalks, the sexes appear to mingle peacefully, without irritation or clashes. They know one another and rub shoulders, accustomed to the neighbor being individually different though looking quite familiar.

The colors of darkness make them lose their urge to sing. What happens when they stop? No doubt they need the silence so that despite the constant contact and perpetual proximity they can finally develop genuine togetherness and much-needed closeness. When you are never apart, bit by bit comes love upon the scene, fostered by what you took at first for the bonds of friendship. Instead, one day, one evening, without your realizing it, suddenly love is there. It stimulates the senses, dilates the heart with a new kind of fever, and leads inevitably to caresses and embraces in the night.

Pressed against the bark, cicadas mate, with the male mounted on his love partner in a repetitive little dance movement. This is the sudden culmination of who or what they are, the door to joys not previously known, and the crowning glory of a single summer; afterward they must die, in the neutral autumn air, when plants are showing their first signs of fading. Only the eggs come through the winter, returning to the world beneath the ground to build up their strength. They are like the ghosts of a brief existence that was squandered, to the accompaniment of clashing cymbals, in the sheer pleasure of being alive.

Loves and Lives of a Millipede

🌿

On the foot-shaped "Japanese stepstones" marking walks and pathways in public gardens, millipedes abound when the hot weather comes. These black-sheathed myriapods roll up the moment you touch them. At the first sign of danger, they instinctively coil into a shell shape, in fact into a shell that we don't see but that may have been theirs in the early stages of their evolution out from the ocean.

They have to make do with a cylindrical body, comprising a number of identical segments. To see them moving, you would think that the segments were retracting into each other, folding in, then extending out, like the sections of a collapsible telescope. The sequence of footsteps produce an inaudible rustling; there are no "blank spaces," just a continuous wave motion passing from leg to leg.

Their head (which conveys an impression of narrow-minded obstinacy) is capsule shaped. It has articulated antennas, and oral appendages that are quite satisfying for anyone who feeds on remnants of plants or, occasionally, a delectable little insect corpse.

When you are a millipede, metamorphosis is required of you at regular intervals as a standard practice, a routine miracle. It's a part of life for millipedes, a prescribed ritual that they must honor, but they do so with confidence and conviction, secure in the knowledge that they will be pleased with the outcome every time.

At some point in their stroll, they come to a stop, halted by an imperious command, a force they cannot resist, which pins them motionless to the earth. Their skin undergoes a circular hardening, forming a coffinlike casing, a curved sheath. The mystery of transformation is acted out in the darkness of this sarcophagus. The millipede drops into an unconscious sleep, a brief miniature death, and, further yet, into what is literally "an entombment in oneself," while the life force oversees his regeneration. When he frees himself from the sheath, having impatiently bored an opening, he regains all his faculties plus a bonus. He returns to active life, to existence and the world, with a burst of renewed energy. The more he molts, the better he gets. The number of double segments increases; the myriapods fill out and show signs of maturity; they grow additional legs, until a fixed number has been reached.

They mate; stimulated by physical contact with a partner, they immediately recover a forgotten sexual fervor that had become dulled as the millipedes trudged along. They have not knowingly sought this captivating urge, but suddenly it hits them, a gift bestowed by life. (Or are we to believe that during the period of their heat, they send out and receive sound signals or particles of scent to alert each other and so be brought together?)

The male does not bother with polite phrases or sophisticated courtship. Courting the female he has met is far from his mind; so is performing a subtle little mating dance in front of her; persuading her to join the dance is further still. He mounts her with no flirtation and no foreplay.

Unlike most of the insects and other garden dwellers, who have their copulatory organ in the posterior portion of their anatomy, the millipede exhibits his at "hip" level, which is to say two-thirds of the way toward the front of his body. Would his pleasure be subtler, or cruder, for being closer to his head? It's anyone's guess, since millipedes make no allowance for whimsy or uncertainty in their sexual relations. Scent-bearing glands operate from one segment to the next, but it is not known whether the myriapods give off this scent for their own benefit during copulation, or whether they give off other, headier fragrances that might be taken for a confused expression of rapture.

However that may be, the millipede does not go into a death agony after coupling, any more than he is devoured by his partner, as seems to be the festive tradition observed by other species. He survives lovemaking very nicely, thank you, and does not appear astonished at the privilege granted him or even particularly grateful. Immediately after the sexual act, however, he does treat himself to another molt.

What we have this time might be called a regressive molt. He comes out a true certified copy of what went in, except that his copulatory organs are now withered, or to be more precise reduced to their previous developmental state. So he has slipped back one notch and is once again the millipede he was before entering his maturational molt.

After an undetermined lapse of time—equivalent to the turbulent teens—he becomes involved in yet another transformation that turns him back into a fully operative male. He is anxious to resume contact with the wide world and, as he ambles along, may go so far as to confuse the dimensions of that world with the sharp outlines of his own sudden desires. He goes back to the same life—but it's a brand-new life, and he has no idea what it holds in store, since in all probability he has no memory of the one before.

The Way to a Bug's Heart

❦

First Bite—The Golden-spotted Carabus

*T*he carabus (or ground beetle) deals expeditiously with love; he just goes ahead, without any preliminary blandishments. No shy curiosity, no maneuvers, no fondling; he just pounces on the first lady carabus who happens along. He cares not a whit about being pleasant or attractive: all he wants is the carnal act, now, at once, and he performs it in a short, sharp straddling of his partner. As soon as a series of jerking movements have culminated in his spilling his seed, off he gets.

The lady ground beetle, her eyes still narrowed from the male's embrace, promptly brings her disordered senses back under control and is instantly assailed by a different sort of hunger, a deep, consuming need that shakes her to the core. It may be that this quick and quasi-anonymous form of copulation brings her not the satisfaction she hoped for but a wrongful, lingering ache. Or it may be that to her, sex is a relatively unimportant affair, even a matter of indifference, like a bridge that has to be crossed, a brief conjugal skirmish that she endures with cold calculation because it's to her advantage.

The event was of such short duration that it could find no echo in her heart; instead, without warning, the dazed female turns into a devouring monster. Love, or some equally unleashed mysterious force, is demanding that she consume the Other. Aside from that, you could say she has a rape to avenge, an unspeakably brutal act of intercourse.

At once she launches herself in pursuit of the male, who is briskly making off, with the carefree satisfaction that comes from a callously stolen pleasure. She quickly overtakes him and, using her legs as a lever, folding them in then extending them out, she tips him over onto his back and holds him pinned in that position, though his legs are flailing frantically, one last time.

Immediately she bores into his stomach and then makes the hole bigger. In a frenzied burst of activity, she tugs, pulls and rips out his entrails, feasting greedily upon them, ingurgitating as she goes along. The banquet is soon over, but her apparent delight in it is a tribute to the partner of a single mating. With meticulous, maniacal care, she picks his belly clean, until it looks like a hollow little brooch from which the sun can still call forth a golden glint. Her appetite does not extend to the corselet, the wing sheaths, the face, or any of the sense organs; all these the female ground beetle leaves intact, in a refinement of funeral pomp.

Confronted with this sexual cannibalism, we are a prey to emotions so conflicting that they amount to a pathology of devourment. To us the motives behind this gluttonous act of cruelty remain at once obscure, unacceptable, monstrous, and mysterious, but perhaps they are none of those things. It just goes to show how a world that is not ours will inevitably have rituals rooted in a "culture" we can never hope to fathom. Our reaction is one of horror, plus a revulsion tinged occasionally with dangerous fascination. The horror is a convulsive manifestation inside *ourselves*, and relates to *ourselves* as members of a civilization that has shut itself off. Within its walls, we have established, once and for all, what things we may properly believe, tolerate, and do.

Perhaps it will help if we realize that the intestines being torn out by the female carabus are the folded, twisted, dark seat of digestion, where the Other, the lover, assimilated and changed what he ate. It's as though she were going out of her way to swallow the very essence of his appetite, to consume his passion and every potential he might have had. She is eating away the very source of his desires, ingesting the long conduit where food was transformed, and "her voracious behavior may appear fearful, nay, frightful to those who dare not confront their own deep animal nature."

Second Bite—The Mantis

If she wants to be admired, the first thing the mantis has in her favor is a clear, delicate, single color verging on apple green. The color has a translucent quality but remains consistently opaque. She is an aesthetic wonder, a proud, confident mystery standing in the light for all to see. Her prayerful posture, arms folded against her chest, gives the impression that she has nothing to hide and that at the same time she harbors no feelings of distrust. Instead, we find that she tends toward thoughtful religious ecstasy, tranquil statements of self, and even an openness of character suited to her extreme purity of form.

She is not merely elegant, she is graceful. Slim waistline, slender, well-articulated arms, a few tiny pearls fastening the bustline. She has a trim figure, with pronounced plumpness in just the right place: that elongated abdomen seems a pledge of lovemaking in a boundless aura of tenderness and understanding, not to mention a promise of successful motherhood. Topping off her adornments are a pair of fine, full, diaphanous wings, shot through with veins that make you think of precious lace. Her wings never serve as organs of flight; they seem rather to be precious regal ornaments, inherited through an ancient lineage of highest rank.

The jade green nontransparent eyes protrude from their sockets to gaze in grave astonishment at all they see. Their roundness seems to take in or encompass the whole world. The greatness of the mantis is that she observes. She is equally intrigued by every location she visits, but first she has to examine, scrutinize, take it all in, until she has grasped all the hidden ramifications. Whereas most species use their visual faculty only to avoid a trap or spy out a lucrative opportunity—some go so far as to disappear into the private parlors of a flower without pausing to notice wonders of the goldsmith's art right before their eyes—the mantis alone is endowed with a sense of observation; she alone is temperamentally suited to contemplation of her surroundings. Wherever she may be, she sets out to form an impression of that place, and her impressions, powerful and clearly defined, are attentive to nuances, slight disturbances, and all the unexpected ways life has of making its presence felt.

From her physical fitness and unabashedly healthy looks, certain militant abstainers or fans of milk products with 0 percent fat content might assume she was a vegetarian. They compare her to young females of our own species who feed exclusively on fruit, cereal flakes, and macrobiotic grains, which gives their faces a permanent glow of rapture, as though they were witnessing some mystic apparition in the midst of a human race that has lost its appetite after mislaying its hunger.

Others, including ourselves, have on the contrary been very pleased to learn that she is a flesh eater, a flesh eater, moreover, with breadth of vision and excellent taste. Not only that: the mantis stands magnificently equipped for her love feasts: witness a double row of serrated knives along the inside of the arms, and splendidly arranged oral appendages. She hunts from ambush, waylaying her prey, counting on camouflage, tactical immobility, and her placid, prayerful posture to take an unsuspecting passerby off-guard. She does not store her kill—the cupboard is bare—but relies on the gifts life may give, the many vagaries of chance, and the imprudent behavior of seasonal game. A few bluebottle flies by way of appetizers, innards of ground beetle or grasshopper legs as a starter course, and finally an ash-colored locust or cross-spider for the entrée. And what will Madame have to drink? A throat-searing morning-dew brandy; just a few drops. And when the feast is over, the mantis folds up again among the plant stalks; there is nothing she likes better than the voluptuous heavy feeling that steals over her while she's digesting.

A male, noticeably smaller than she, has caught sight of the female. When he spots her with her limbs folded in a particular way, motionless, blending with the striped green of the grasses, the first thing he does is freeze. He makes his approach in slow motion, bit by tiny bit, putting one leg forward, then another, with strategic halts, long intervals when movement is suspended.

He would like not to be noticed until too late, when he's already at it. He circles the lady, thinking what a clever fellow he is, what a keenly perceptive chap. He stops once again, this time in midmotion, as though he were trying in advance to escape a deadly peril. That delicate green color worn by his intended reassures him; so does the sight of her abdomen, which has dilated further: the ovaries are maturing the eggs as mating time draws near; it's as if the male's imminent pleasure were assuming greater compass. He has now entered the hermetically sealed zone where attractions are irresistible and precautions a thing of the past.

Thus far the female has remained prostrate in a position of strict, pious worship, lost in silent sanctity. And very likely her religiosity heightens the male's primitive pagan lust, as the act he is contemplating takes on a suggestion of sacrilege.

At a sign of consent from the female, he comes up to her, takes a deep breath to gather his fiery strength, bows his head, raises it, turns it this way and that, and finally puffs out his chest in a show of virility.

With no preliminaries, no kisses or tender touching, no delicious nibbles at the nape of her neck or the sensitive hollow of her loins, up he climbs onto her back; he hangs on, gets a grip, and mating begins. It will not end for nearly two hours.

That promising abdomen has in no way misled him: he is unhurriedly reaping the benefits of his boldness.

But while he holds her in his embrace, completely absorbed by his task, the female raises her pincers and applies them expertly to her partner's neck. He is expecting an additional embrace, some special erotic play or insistent stroking to be understood as a sign of encouragement, but suddenly a splatter of red spurts up into his eyes and he lapses instantly into total unconsciousness: with a stroke of her serrated knife, his mistress has just cut off his head. And despite this, the rest of his body goes on with the mating.

Having lost his head, it's as though all he has left is sex, the moment of seminal fire that has to be achieved, but now minus the complications caused by fantasizing, minus the inevitable orchestrated feelings, minus those mood swings that so often get in the way of action, to the point where action may be thwarted by sudden attacks of impotence.

While he presses on with what he was doing, going in deeper and deeper to release his seed, the female mantis continues to hack away the nape of his neck, then his chest, in a succession of bites. She swallows him up with a perseverance that does her credit. Having once started to devour, she is determined to see the job through to the end. It would be hard to imagine a warmer welcoming of Other into Self; an appetite such as hers compels admiration. This goes beyond an act of taking possession; this is a genuine instance of absorbing the Other, who will be subjected to a lengthy process of digestion. Then the mantis will once again enjoy the voluptuously heavy feeling she experiences after her feasts, only this time the feeling is of higher quality because it includes love.

When her amorous appetite is satisfied, the only portion of her partner she has not eaten is the wings. Why the wings? Are they not to her taste? Are they hard to digest? Left to dry out rapidly or be attacked by rain, the wings dissolve into shining dust, a bit of powder that disappears the way memory disappears from the scene of their nuptials.

Sparks in the Dark of Night

✿

*A*t summer solstice, the triangle of stars formed by Vega, Deneb, and Altair dominates the midnight sky. Then you may pick out, from the multitude, Arcturus of the constellation Plow and the Spike of Grain in Virgo, while Scorpio's Antares is to the south. At such times the shadows on the ground seem less well defined and less interwoven; their outlines are softer and fleecier, with velvety depths. There are emanations from the fruit and flowers; warmth is reflected silently back from the stones, which have stored it up all day. As a result, the night seems thinned out, the darkness gentler, more open and welcoming.

This is the hesitant beginning of maturation season, a count-down mechanism housed in nature's pulp and sap. Everywhere an immense force is stirring, exuding a peace you can almost feel, like a woman's suntanned flesh, smooth to your touch, with a smoothness extending to each atom of her body. Every sense perception and every thought is filled with a slow but omnipresent and persistent resonance. Though our senses perceive no motion, the vibrations continue, uninterrupted and signifying growth. The inviolable border between worlds is finally blurring, and the great concave mirror of knowledge is imperceptibly losing its power to reflect.

When the garden lies relaxed in a deep untroubled sleep, from its ebony shadows lights like stars begin to twinkle, "pale gold teardrops that the moon has shed." Some of the lights sparkle intermittently and move in zigzag lines, level with the branches of the elder; others are in the grass, anchored to the ground, like landing lights. What new constellations have we here, calling, beckoning, answering one another?

These scattered signals—broadcast from the enchanted show put on by the glowworms—seem to compose a mysterious message, but in our bewitched state we feel no great urge to decode it right away. The code is keyed to a midsummer night's dream. The twinkling is part of a magic spell, a series of little candlelights softly tinged with blue, set against a dark page. On either side of the page is a void, and there are other horizon lines nearby, part of a depth perspective we had forgotten in our vague impression that we had blended with our surroundings till they and we were as one.

Throughout her life, the female glowworm retains a larval appearance, as though she had stopped and been caught between metamorphoses. She is ill-favored, and although she belongs to the Coleoptera family, she will never grow wings or know the intoxicating freedom of flight. Her six short legs are her only means of transport, but they do enable her to pitter-patter along.

Her field of inquiry is the ground, whether between the plant stalks, or ground that has been dug up, or the rough surface of bare earth. In such a lowly state she needs to attract attention, send out semaphore signals, put on a display of irregularly flashing lights. She issues a call for pairing. To give her flashes of white a wide distribution, she does contortions; she twists the tip of her belly, turning it this way and that, until she captures the attention of a male on the prowl up there and summons him to take part in a wedding down here.

What a fascinating performance and what magnificent strategy! The female behaves as though she were aware of her disadvantaged status, aware that she is unprovided with allurements or adornments and that her body could never hope to tempt anyone. So she waits for the night, when she can make her long, unattractive shape hard to distinguish among the grasses, and then she dons a splendid belt of light. This is her shining lamp, the halo around her desires, the luminous radiance of the only seduction she can muster. We are reminded of those lanterns hung out in the night to guide love-starved strangers walking the roads, wandering aimlessly, their loins on fire, calling out every step of the way to the sweetheart they are frantic to have, while somewhere she, too, is wandering or lingering in horrible loneliness.

Up to the present, the male, wearing an uncomfortably tight uniform of mixed brown and mahogany, has been leading a similar larval existence. But with the approach of the pairing-off season, and the ardor stirred in him by a powerful, mysterious urge that dilates his senses as it gets stronger, he thinks: *If I had wings, I'd fly*. And he does indeed grow wings. Just when the firebrand of love is goading him on, he develops a taste for nighttime explorations, a lust for heights, dizzy cravings for adventure. Flying over the countryside, at low altitude, his attention is suddenly drawn to a little concerto of light.

This signal, blinking in a code known only to him and which he instantly deciphers, is enough to tell him that the female is in a very receptive mood. He lands quickly and, after some confusion, is soon locked in lovemaking. So feeble is the prevailing light, that the lovers' faces appear softly transfigured; they look unreal, almost mystical. The light is from the dimmed lantern of their hindmost segment, left on by the pair of lovers "to keep discreet watch over their nuptials."

Spider-Woman and the Kiss of Death

❧

*A*s soon as her web is spun, she stations herself at the place set aside for waiting. She is on the lookout, perfectly still; her keen gaze gives no hint of her emotions. She makes her mind, indeed her whole self, a perfect blank. Her nerves are stretched thin with all this watchfulness, this constant tension. At least her belly feels better, relieved of all the silk used in building her trap. She drew the strand out as it was needed. First she anchored a great many mooring posts in the grass and brush, dropping down by double rope, then climbing back up, knotting, weaving, setting strands crosswise, and interlacing her moist threads with a kind of glue, all the while working out from the center with a pedaling motion of her eight legs.

Crouched like a hunter whose slightest movement might betray his presence to the birds, she attunes herself to any suggestion of swaying in her web. It is her fate to spend much of her life waiting, and to pass the time she meditates endlessly. What does a spider ponder about, supposing a spider to ponder? Obviously about the game she may trap, her preferences in prey, and chance offerings of tasty items that she hasn't previously sampled. But maybe, in addition to these hunger-inspired dreams of splendid catches, maybe she gives way to rose-colored feminine reveries, magic-mirror stuff with sentimental complications and concerns. Eyes wide open, she spins a dream that starts out vague but then focuses more and more on the hidden figure of the lover who sooner or later must appear, to be caught in the threads she has spun.

She waits; she will not succumb to anguish and despair when she thinks there must have been delays. She is expecting an arrival, the approach of a visitor, a prearranged signal, an unmistakable quiver of the web that will bring her rushing out to see what creature she has caught, bind the captive with silk, and sink her fangs into his chest or the nape of his neck. She's busy with her calculations and trying not to let things get out of proportion. Any matter that interests her is immediately considered in terms of symmetry and geometric figures. She draws up estimates, consults the oracles when wind sets her web vibrating, avoids errors, and rejects the suggestion of shattered dreams or a lover who didn't keep a tryst. She has her moments of gloom and depression. She waits. Everything in her orbit strikes her as inane, futile, and unreal. Her legs remain perfectly still while she goes through all sorts of moods. Colors come to fill the neutral emptiness of waiting: the fluid tones of enchantment, then the chalky blackness of derision or despair, and finally the reddish bursts of delirium. Drawing on her capacity for love, she endlessly creates and re-creates the uncertain outline of that expected lover. Desire takes on shape, substance, and identity simply because she is so sure that he is the one she's been waiting for and she is the one he's been waiting for. Only she can't help being a little frightened at how long it is taking him to appear, make himself known, and immolate himself to love.

At last! after many a futile, sometimes desperate attempt to find the web, he is coming her way. The watchful, waiting female, four times his size and with eyesight to match, has already spotted him. Just a tawny velvet dot emerging from nowhere, down among the interwoven leaves of grass. The dot is moving steadily in her direction. It swells, enlarges, settles into the familiar outline of a not particularly large abdomen, with the usual eight legs radiating out from underneath. For her, the approach of any creature is initially suspect and possibly dangerous, even if the promise that tonight there'll be food aplenty gets more and more substantial as the creature comes closer. Aplenty and then some; she keeps silk-swathed packaged food in the cupboard for a rainy day: the torso of a moth, grasshopper legs, or a few plain two-winged flies with their black metallic glint. But today's venturesome visitor isn't exactly prey; he is something more, something glorious and hard to describe, sharpening her senses and producing a lazy, loving lethargy. For the moment, however, she remains prudent, almost diplomatic. There exists a different kind of providence for a different kind of gratification, pleasures more subtle, more fertile.

He, meanwhile, intends to take his chances with this trap, which seems to him an extension and protection of the coveted female. He wastes no time admiring the airy, daring, soaring architecture, as fine as it is effective. The web is there, a perfect structure, with the dew adding a thin gloss that emphasizes each strand. Extended in a vertical or nearly vertical plane, it suggests a net for sophisticated acrobatics.

With naive eagerness he tugs at one of the guy-strands as if he were tugging at a bellpull for someone to come and let him in. He is making the web vibrate in one direction, not like the frantic, broken rhythm of a victim struggling in the threads. His desire is suddenly quickened when he catches sight of its object, four times larger than he and acting in a very practical, decisive manner compared to his own timid behavior.

At a sign of acquiescence from the female, he plucks up courage, while she comes down to meet him, lowering herself by double rope. As they near one another, she turns so that the most sensitive part of her abdomen is facing her suitor. At the same time, she makes occasional pedaling motions with her legs, two by two. There is something provoking and macabre, hence attractive, about this nuptial dance. Clearly she is inviting him to mate, but a threatening atmosphere hangs over the invitation.

Little by little, he comes closer. His hypnotic state translates into a steady oscillating movement that is communicated to the shining trap of the web. The attraction has become irresistible. The male stretches his two anterior pairs of legs out in front of him, freezes in that position, and seems to weigh up his chances of success. Then he holds out the leg that carries his encapsulated seed. He is making the requisite offering, and she graciously approves.

Immediately he leaps onto her, tries to hang on, falls in a heap off to one side, grabs a double strand to steady himself and gives himself a shake. Recovering his senses, he performs his courtship routine a second time, holds out the same leg, climbs back aboard, and finally contrives to poke his sperm pouch into the orifice, which has been lubricated for his convenience.

In the course of his endeavors, the male has been forced to assume a position that brings his abdomen level with the love partner's oral appendages and, notably, level with her fangs, which she at once jabs into his flesh. In so doing, she is reverting instinctively to all her usual reactions and inhibitions. The effect of this poisoned kiss, which could have been merely pleasurable, is to send the lover almost instantly into a coma. He will not come out of it.

Sometimes the male succeeds in dodging, but only to be caught in the sticky threads, and the harder he tries to free himself the more he gets enmeshed. She ties him up with her ropes of silk before administering the fatal kiss as a coup de grace. After paying due homage to her, after bestowing on her all that was in his power to bestow, the male is of no further use now that a certain desire has been satisfied, and he is about to provide the makings of a feast.

In the irresistible attraction drawing him urgently to a female spider who will slay him with her fangs, there resides an extreme of cruelty and blind cannibalism serving no purpose. The female's appetite could be amply satisfied with other prey, after all. It would be more to her advantage if she took this lover whose career has barely begun and recycled him as a household husband.

The World of the Stick Insects

✣

*I*f you gently thrust your hand into the undergrowth, at no particular place, you may detect his presence as he suddenly, in spite of himself, jerks his leg away—which is not his customary behavior: whatever may threaten him, his response is almost invariably to stay stock-still and be indistinguishable.

By virtue of his spindly, elongated body, structured like the twigs on which he perches, the walkingstick (one of the phasmids) achieves perfect mimicry. The undergrowth is scaled to his size and serves as a forest. He betakes himself to a leafy or thorny shrub, there to assume his post as the continuation of a tiny branch stump or an addition to the green bower. Even his shadow is lost in the complex, tangled shade of this sunscoured bushland.

He chooses a perch, changes his color to match the twig's, and hangs there, not revealing anything of his inner self. Nothing filters through, no hint of what's on his mind at the moment, no clue to his anxieties, hostilities, fears, or delights, to say nothing of thoughts and feelings that it might be a little difficult to credit him with. He is simply there, narrow and impenetrable. Some small occurrence will suddenly make him reveal his presence; his body will move sharply and for a brief moment be distinct from the twig, but for the most part his ambition is not to stand out. His being there tells you nothing, and perhaps there is nothing to tell. It's as though he were in fact a bit of underbrush that had somehow been imbued with a stronger, basically foreign vitality.

The phasmid never goes anywhere except at night, and never very far even then. He comes back to his favorite post; or else he chooses another, at a new place that catches his fancy and strikes him as suited to his nature. In the dense criss-cross of branches, he makes for the base of the growth, seeking out bits of vegetation just starting to rot. These he consumes with great relish, even indulging in a few unaccustomed body movements under cover of the conniving darkness. Both going and coming, he journeys with utmost wariness and caution. There are silences, halts, and prolonged pauses in his motions, making them appear disjointed, but doubtless they are imprinted with their own inner rules of harmony.

Clinging to his perch in the scrub, he appears oblivious or indifferent to his surroundings—as if he were mimicking them so perfectly that even his inner life is totally erased—and yet he belongs to our world and no other, future or bygone. It's not as though he had boundaries to cross. He tests the texture of things by melting into them and melding with them. A tiny fragment of forest moving about. A fragment of forest anchored to the axil of the branches.

All around him are pools of light, pockets of shadow, the bustling of wings, cries and vibrations, confused noises, sounds

of twigs snapping, undefined patches in the amazing assort-
ment of greens that mingle deep in the plant fibers. None of it
escapes his attention. If something stirs that shouldn't, if a
shadow starts to get bigger, if there is the slightest forewarning
of danger, he knows. But he spies without betraying his presence. Possibly, underneath the stiff posture (posturing, really)
that he adopts on all occasions, his tactical immobility leads
him to be overanxious, prone to suspicion, and continuously
on the alert. With a few stretches of his spindly legs, he casts
off each successive molt as one casts off an old coat. He
emerges from the molt to find his world, the world he has been
part of since the day he was born, identical to what it was
before. Showing no sign of astonishment, he picks up his life
of mimicry at the point where it was interrupted by a brief,
pointless metamorphosis.

Love comes at last. The walkingstick is made aware of its
coming by a kind of stealthy warming around his body, frantic
fits of shivering, and a rapid dilation of his private parts. Till
now, he has been leading an unremarkable existence with limited desire, discreetly modest day-to-day appetites, and no
thought of a possible erotic side to his nature. But now the magnetic attraction in his blood is becoming more pronounced, and
the excitement of his flesh is rousing him to ecstatic heights, as
though he really were the extension of a twig in the underbrush
and bubbling, frothing sap were flowing from the twig into him.

With his jointed, awkward gait (but it looks more sprightly
now), he buries himself in among the stalks of grass and hun-
kers down in the shade, where he can be sure no one will spy
on him or pounce on him. He needs some time to himself,
freedom to let himself go, become familiar with his desires and

make room in his ethos for the sensual pleasures ahead. His reproductive processes work by parthenogenesis, in the secrecy of a gynoecium that has its own little ways, its own fluid, fertile forces. The phasmid does not indulge in any sort of mating or other intrusive intimacy, even though he belongs to a sexed species. Fertilization results from a kind of unrequited embrace deep down in the flesh, and the pleasure curves up on itself, as if to concentrate and intensify its delicately subtle quality.

PART

III

Frothy Wedding

❧

*T*he snails are out. As soon as the bright hatchings of rain had stopped, snails, their horns pricked up, were everywhere to be seen.

A long way off, mists are lifting—especially along the road that winds into the hills—and closer by, thin vapors also rise, as when varnish is drying; they expand, thin out, and disappear. A golden yellow sun, meanwhile, shakes off the haze and goes back to rummaging in the garden. The world is fluid, shimmering, unsubstantial; its contours dissipate as in dreams, against an extraordinary blend of light and water.

Everything sparkles. Light is gleaming, flashing, refracting, brilliantly shining. Molten glass flows in thin streams over the leaves. Water dripping. Trickling. All this splendor is fragmented, scattered like a broken mirror, so that pieces reflect even from the clumps of rosemary, the extravagant growth of sage, and the cathedraled darkness of the grass leaves lying collapsed upon each other.

Who can describe the ease and freedom flowing from fluidity? When it has rained, the snail can crawl, glide, move, without having to dribble too much of the damp secretion that lubricates his path as he goes along. Shell brightly polished, he stretches out, leans to one side, maneuvers, his body long and moist, flowing over the crushed teardrops of the rain shower. Besides which, the cooler air all around is giving him an appetite, a fresh start, a mind once more serene and freed from care, and muscles toned like new. How could it be otherwise, when about him rise and hover odors of ozone and good, macerating smells of garden humus hacked open by the rain?

Ordinarily, snails lead a nighttime life, dozing by day in a cleft of their choosing—the crevice in a garden wall, the hollow of a root—in detritus of plants or under the rusted leaves of Virginia creepers. Occasionally they assemble in family groups, where their shells range from the most mature to the most minute, a set of nesting snails, as though you could slide one inside the other. But should a shower come, assailed by raindrops that are often cold, they emerge from their lethargic memory-free sleep, elongate, stretch out from their helical habitat to full length, and unfold the stalks supporting their eyes. The rain is calling them. Sharpening their senses and their appetite, the odor-filled opened-out watery world invites them to venture forth along the ever familiar footpaths leading onward into the unknown.

One of them has found refuge under a Roman tile that someone left leaning against a retaining wall. The snail fastens himself to the tile for his periods of rest, a fat spiral welded by a kind of thick, dried saliva that cracks like dried glue every time he wakes and stirs.

The whorl that bedecks and hollows his shell has the fascination of an ancient, archetypal motif. It speaks of first origins;

it must surely be or contain a basic, obvious secret, maybe even telling us how we should understand the development of our own existence. The whorl revolves out from the center around a fixed pole, a coiled expansion that the science of symbolics has interpreted as "a universally understood glyph of temporality, indicating the continuity of being, through all the fluctuations of change."

Aside from his shell, the snail's shape suggests merely an elongated foot, flattened to a fleshy disk, with states of motion flowing along it in unison. It crawls, retracts, expands, and advances with movements of the whole body. Prolonged tremors travel the length of the foot, wave motions generated by a series of muscular contractions, causing undulations that go from the back to the front. The snail's secretion generously lubricates a mechanism that produces a loosening out followed by a drawing in of the parallel folds, coordinated clenching followed immediately by unclenching. (I have attempted a dozen times to write up, no, to write down, at any rate to write rightly of the wonderful way the snail walks. I have tried to write from nature, letting his movements burn their way into my consciousness, then, in a kind of alliterary effort, through repetition of consonants and the ricochet of vowels, compelling the words to assume a sort of muffled, crawling effect, a slow-tempo progression, a steady, peaceful succession of expansions and retractions allowing the snail to flow along his slimy path.)

Well, there he is, strolling along with practiced, placid ease. He slides over things, adapting to their contours, goes around obstacles or across them, coiling up and lengthening out. Sometimes he senses a danger or a breach, as though he were coming to a footbridge that had collapsed or a road with a cave-in. When that happens, anxiety and uncertainty vie for possession of his soul. He rears slightly up, expresses extra slime, and rolls his horns around to show he doesn't understand. First he retracts, then he acts as if he's going to give it a try, then he huddles into his shell. He prudently reappears after an unspecified lapse of time, unfolds his eyestalks, reappraises himself and the world, and resolutely resumes his wayfaring, heading where his gluttony leads. He leaves behind a shiny, odoriferous track that will enable him to find his way home, retrace his steps without becoming lost, and get back to his special shelter. Upon his return, he will stick himself to that tile again with a bit of froth.

That very morning a few drops of rain had splattered him, and he woke up grasping at the wisps of a dream. He wishes he could remember how the dream turned out, who was in it and all the details, as if it involved a puzzle that wanted solving, an annunciation whose significance he needed to grasp. He stretches outside his shell to work off a bit of stiffness or traces of sleep in his muscle tissue. The dream may have fled, but it has left a kind of whitish magnetism still floating around in his mind; there's a vague dizziness, an undefinable something drawing him in and driving him wild; it's all immensely disturbing. He must go out, this very moment, get back to the world outside the tile, back to his silvery, slippery paths. He has the illusion of moving along faster than usual, though not as fast as he would like. He feels as though he were about to be late for an encounter and miss an opportunity that might never be offered again.

He has already progressed farther than the feeding ground where he customarily gnaws and devours everything in sight, leaving a lacework of successive bites. He bypasses some young shoots of seeded grain, a treat that would normally stop him cold. Nor does he evince any interest in the white lily he had started to strip down to the stalk. (On that particular greedy raid he'd worked with a number of lily-loving associates.) He pursues his journey in almost glorious determination, and we get the impression that an unfocused impatience has replaced his usual appetites.

By now he is boldly going where no snail, at any rate not this one, has gone before, and there is an absence of familiar landmarks. This is new territory, a far place that of course has always been there and where everything happens as it does at home. The rain has left the same streams of molten glass, the same drops of pewter glinting from the grasses. It was a fluid frontier, and he crossed it without even noticing. But the air he is breathing strikes him as more evanescent and somehow alcoholic.

At the mouth of a narrow passage through the grass stalks, where mists are dispersing, another snail is likewise moving along, in a similar mood, with his thoughts still jumbled from a morning dream and a magnetic attraction like a diffused burning in his flesh. They catch sight of one another, and each immediately reads his own desire in the desire of the other, as though everything was already taking place through mirror image and in duplicate. Slow motion now reigns supreme, time stretches out, lazy enjoyment is the order of the day. The attraction, however, is immediate, covetous complicity is established from the outset, and the new association is already an amorous one. Around them, the world they have stopped observing continues to shatter in the faceted splendor of liquid cristal.

Their encounter takes place with a few anemones for witness, on a narrow strip of granular earth that is still soaking wet. The rain used transparent elastic threads to stitch the first light of dawn into the sleep-fuddled flesh of night. The two snails sail closer, on a long, voluptuous collision course. But before they turn on their sides, before they align their fleshy feet and weld them in a frothy bath using a festooned arrangement of suckers, they indulge in foreplay. Preparatory touches are exchanged, preliminary titillation, prefatory arousal. The shells dance. The horns roll up. They stroke each other with a mutual rubbing and crossing of their pedicles; the pedicle stems almost intertwine. The snails retract them in sudden embarrassment and also to postpone pleasure that is probably too intense. They substitute a series of light contacts, extending the pedicles once again, and tenderly, insistently touching each other, especially around the eyes.

This ballet of love, which has an airy grace to it, lasts a long time, and even longer for the gastropods than it would be for us, since our space-time grid is not the same. It seems, too, that they wouldn't want to ruin part of the enjoyment through giddy eagerness, pushing and shoving or skipping stages in their haste to reach the goal. They have no call to proceed any faster than they intended, nor to outrun their own desires, nor to rush headlong toward the objective.

Meanwhile, they have begun to exchange bites 'n' kisses on the neck and along the torso. As their tongue is covered with thousands of minuscule rough spots that make it into more of a grater than a tongue, those kisses can hurt! But when your skin is the skin of a mollusk, timid titillations, light massaging, and even the cleverest caresses would not get you very far.

What the snails need to do is nibble, bite, prick, prod, pinch, and painfully snag all that unresponsive muscle tissue. And, of course, be bitten, nibbled, et cetera, right back—pricked till their flesh responds, snagged in turn by the partner's kisses at their throat.

Could the harm we freely do increase the good we receive? A score of sharp, insistent, irritating little stabs of pain, verging on pleasure, broaden the bounds of feeling that are normally benumbed. Passionately biting here, there, and everywhere, what the snails achieve is to waken the whole geography of sensation, the whole map of their receptivity. One after another they stimulate every sensory point on the other's body, inflame the other's erogenous zones, as if each needed to pinpoint the susceptible area in himself where the double embrace of their coupling is going to be carried out. Thus a quest for pleasure, and an instinct entrusted with perpetuating the species, team up to open new roads and conquer unsuspected regions in the flesh. All for the benefit of a great, overmastering desire that the snails never doubt their ability to satisfy. Perhaps, too, this strategy is the simple foundation on which they build a structure of feelings and sense perceptions that are not simple at all, but complex and refined.

By now, each has rolled on his side, and they are joined by the soles of their feet. They clasp one another along their edges, roll and unroll with a greater output of slime, then go at it again, embracing, hugging, and using suction to bind their bodies more closely yet. In response to other stimuli, every time they retract and then stretch out, more froth is expressed. They discover that their reaction one to the other makes them voluptuously viscous, amazingly able to twist and twine; the euphoria filling their muscle tissue lifts them to a plane of absolute delight.

Two halves join to form a bivalve. Two sexes are mixed, two are mingled. And since each snail is both male and female, each is at once she who is penetrated, he who penetrates. Not for them the silver or golden but the frothy wedding, when two creatures devote themselves to the labor of love with great fervor and equally great sensory skill. Each of them immediately experiences what the other is feeling, to such a degree that they could take one another's place and be quite unsurprised. They wouldn't perhaps even notice anything odd about the exchange, since both are commingled to form anew the spiral from which the universe first sprang.

Who was it that wrote of "the double embrace from which they can disengage only at the cost of tearing themselves painfully away, each now bearing the sperm and eggs laid by the other, each a mother and father both, each progenitor and progeny, each getting and got with child, in a combining of combined sexes and the double identity of Other in Self"?

Barbed Love Meets Love Barb

🌿

*T*he scene of another double embrace was the point where a rocky flagging met a clump of sage, the sage-brush almost silvering the shadow it cast. The weather had been steadily fine for several days: a warm drying wind was blowing from the south, the sky was wide open and unstreaked with cloud, mineral blue turning chalky around the hills. To reach the scene from their separate directions, both slugs had been forced to put out substantial amounts of slimy excretion, lubricating their way from earth to dry grass.

They had already reached the stage of gazing at each other close up, either with affected shyness or genuine last-minute reservation. The excessive modesty of A may have struck B (and vice versa) as covering up unwholesome secrets or point-less resistance or provocative indecision. Unless, of course, each of them was trying to guess how much of his anticipated pleaure would turn out to be unexpectedly painful, and equally trying to feel comfortable with the nearly perfect mirror image of self reconstituted in the physical appearance of the other.

The first, very cautious contact consisted of touching horns. These cold-blooded creatures, slow-moving and slow to be moved, require serious stimulation before they wake up to the possibility of amorous doings. They began systematically palpating one another with their pedicles. And so, by dint of rubbing, caressing more insistently, and becoming partly entwined, they were roused little by little to a troubling, mysterious, increasingly sensual state, in which ephemeral dreams seemed to be prolonged by the trembling of their flesh.

Like the snails, they worked up to biting each other on the throat and the side of the head, where the breathing orifices of the pallial cavity are located. (The cavity is their lung.) First there were brief nibbles, then quick pinches, then the bites got more daring, started going deeper and lasting longer, so that the mutual arousal was heightened. There is probably a persistent element of anxiety in such enjoyment as long as self-abandon is not one hundred percent. But our two creatures seemed to be at it body and soul. In the process, they were broadening their sensorial horizons and leaving behind the ordinary dualist idea of pain versus pleasure. With growing excitement, they were venturing further and further toward an unexplored area of their inner being.

Shivers and shudders began to run the length of the "hairy foot" they use for a body. Retracting, stretching, then coiling up, now coiling round. Waves were spreading, originating in spasms of muscular tension that caused undulations to flow from back to front. These wave motions passed right on through into the partner, who would send them rippling back with perfect sympathetic coordination.

Now the bites became more violent, especially when the slugs began rearing up so they could strike more effectively. Any time they needed fresh inspiration, the bright red of their increasingly humid coat could supply it. They must surely have been delighted to discover in each other a great hunger analogous to their own, a twin and growing desire amply attested by thrusts, bites, successive bursts of passion and a characteristic curling of the "foot."

They began frothing even more. Almost certainly the only motive for this generous output of moist secretion is to provide for total ease during the fast-approaching moment of ecstasy. It would indeed be a shame if their satisfaction, which has not reached its peak, were to be marred by inadequate oiling of their parts.

Lubricated to their liking, they embraced, with a violent mutual adhesion at the soles of their feet. They rolled upon the grainy ground, writhing, going through a complex sequence of movements, pressing out then sucking in, all the while probing one another with their pedicles. They swayed their horns this way and that, still eager but now more expert, the pleasure they received informing them what pleasure they should give back for the lover to enjoy.

One of the pair got shaken up, rolled over, jolted, and finally thrown into the shade of the sage plants by his partner, who then hauled him or her back into the light. After the briefest pause, during which he appeared to gather his wits and recover his senses, he coiled up, stretched out full length and darted back into the amorous affray, adapting to the form of embrace being offered by the other. They were once again rolling rapturously about, when suddenly both of

them drew back looking like a grimacing pair of thick lips—
in what the onlooker could only assume was a horrible pang
of pain.

Close to the sex organs (which are double) is a small hidden
pouch. It houses a sharp-pointed hole-boring terebra that science has endowed with the Latin name *Spiculum amore*, meaning, if you please, "Love barb." This miniature limestone
harpoon is brought out the moment the slugs unite. The sting-
ing dart pierces the love partner at her tenderest spot, inflict-
ing an atrociously sharp pain that does not stop. The victim,
similarly armed, reacts in the same extreme fashion, as she in
turn propels her dart into the other's flesh.

So the effect is mutual: pain in equals pain out. Nor is this
piercing agony confined to the point of entry; the neuralgic
paroxysm spreads wherever the nerve tissue takes it. The pain
generalizes to assume a continuous, encircling, concentric pattern, adding contrast and unexpected intensity to the ecstatic
pleasure of the embrace.

A sexual relationship that is inherently hurtful may run
counter to our morality and seem baffling, dark, and revolt-
ing—unless perhaps we make an effort to understand, by looking at ourselves. We have to ask, and answer, questions about
the perverse impulses and the inevitable need for cruelty that
arise in our sexual relations, like marks of mutual esteem.

In the case of the slugs, however, it is more appropriate to
speak of a "going beyond," of something that has to be endured
in order to reach a higher level. The pain is of limited duration
and acts as an agent of self-transcendence. Apparently it is
indispensable if the capacity of the slugs to feel pleasure, and
the map of erogenous zones where they feel it, are to be

increased and enlarged: as has already been said, these creatures are cold by temperament and not readily moved. They have to pierce each other's thick, rubbery flesh in order to provoke sensation. The "love barb" intensely sharpens their mutual receptivity, baring their inner flesh for the fundamental act they have now to perform.

And so they have come together, with the edges of their bodies festooned and hunched up like little puppet figures. The slime is flowing ever more freely, as if they were reproducing between them a little of the foam from some distant sea that no longer exists even in memory. The slugs are hermaphrodites. Tightly bound by their barbs, they begin to mingle their genital organs. At no time does this mean inverted sex, but rather true double exchange in which an individual penetrates and is penetrated at the same time, makes love and equally is made love to. The partners act by turns as female or male, and their intimate structure is such as to make any homosexual relationship impossible. Each slug fecundates the other while being fecundated by the other, and when giving pleasure is simultaneously rewarded with the very same pleasure. The female side takes over the ardent fervor of the male side, which in turn experiences the parallel sensation of being impregnated.

Here is Unity regained, original fusion, impossible double identity at last reborn. Anything the imagination might conjure up is superfluous, fantasizing is simply not there, when two partners are so perfectly, completely, doubly equipped, and when their reciprocal passion is fed by the same inclinations and desires.

Part
IV

Out-of-Body Fertilization

❧

For Maryvonne Verdier
with affectionate good humor

*T*he earth quakes, heaves, bursts, splits into shadowed crevices; and since your gaze is entirely drawn to the exact location of this seismic disturbance—near that trough full to the brim with rainwater—your view of the toad's reappearance is a close-up. He emerges from a shallow, temporary tomb, from cramped, low-roofed darkness, from the drowsiness of a lethargic, slow-moving, probably starless existence.

The movements he makes, to shake off the earth still hampering his limbs, suggest numbness and lack of coordination. He has appeared out of the ground like an aborted misshapen god, the nameless creature of someone's morbid imagination. His lineaments are crudely carved: his head is broad, his body squat, tailless and studded with warts. But who knows, maybe this apparition, so monstrous at first sight, holds imprisoned a Prince Charming for the maiden who succeeds in casting off the evil spell. It happens in fairy tales, after all: the kiss of an innocent dove bestowed upon the slavering toad might well bring the Prince back to life, freeing him from that crouched thickset body with its mud and bronze consistency.

Whatever fills us with revulsion or, worse still, with loathing, is almost always "the door nearest to what we are," a cold attic window looking out over the muddy darkness housed within our selves, the stuff of which we are made, but a darkness in which our good angel is at work, trying to overcome appearances. This is the mud in which our body has cast its mold, and filaments of its filth still hang from us, ready to rise again and mingle with our deepest thoughts, our buried memories, and the far reaches of our imagination. But new ideas, changes as yet unknown, inventions of the mind, recaptured truths, these things also must be born or reborn from shapelessness and chaos. So, too, must ancient memories, imprinted in us long before our birth and erased, we thought, forever.

Experience teaches that we are better off if we domesticate our loathings and better off still if we turn them into allies. When something is so ugly that it fills us with revulsion, we are wise to look closely and carefully, very closely and very carefully indeed, till we detect attractive features and often fascinating patterns in the ugliness. Thus, for instance, to the extent that a toad may sit still long enough to be scrutinized under a magnifying glass, his "wart-studded" skin turns out to be a moonscape curved back on itself, with strange craters and brilliances. It's like the far side of the moon that no one has ever seen but everyone has tried to guess at and describe. All these features are set into somber colors—sea green, wormwood gray, dark green—brighter on the stomach with a kind of rust or moist ocher hue. The bumps flash like a diadem when the light plays on them, bringing out all sorts of mysterious speckles. Even the creature's eye, under magnification, seems to hide deep, secret recesses, the golden refulgences of a light from beyond the grave or atmosphere effects such as one sees in the canvases of Odilon Redon.

When moving about, the toad displays a sure sense of direction; he detects the prey he is about to catch, as unerringly as if he were guided from within by some kind of radar, sending out shortwave signals and picking them up when they bounce back to him from the objects of his gluttony. His head pivots like the gun turret on a tank, firing his tongue to capture prey whose position he has located well in advance.

Then he poses like the king of the castle, sitting back on his folded rear legs. He puffs himself up to add to his importance, gazing unblinkingly at the world with grave unconcern that does not, however, preclude his remaining alert.

To become what he is now, he had to cross the forbidden frontier between water and air, switch from the tadpole's system of breathing through gills to the mature toad's system of breathing mainly through all the pores in the skin, a system charmingly called cutaneous respiration. It's as though he had two distinct and separate lives with no apparent communication between them. He probably hasn't retained any memory of his life as a tadpole, of swimming in a highly charged environment, of being curious about this or that, of being frightened when a carp was dodging back and forth in the silty bottoms or fishing-spiders ran across the glass surface of the pond without even scratching it. He would play with the glass beads that other spiders, water-spiders these, draped over themselves like diving-bells before going down below the surface. Looking up at his tadpole sky, he watched the dance of the dragonflies darting about in a blue, sun-filled world beyond, a world he absurdly aspired to enter. Lastly, he had to dodge a goodly number of predatory attacks, perils that most of his friends did not escape; otherwise they, too, would presumably be alive and among us today.

Aside from breathing through his pores, the toad builds up a supply of air in the vocal sacs housed inside his cheeks. As "vocal sacs" implies, it would appear that this air is used chiefly for singing. In the night, the toad issues his short metallic note. If you listen more closely, the song has its harmonics, its modulations and varied frequencies, liquid resonance effects with lyric countertenor passages. The actual croaking comes as a shock, a real break in the musical unity: starting off rounded and sweet, the sound is brutally cut into by a deep, choking clamor.

During the love season, this sexual attraction does not carry very far. If his song goes unanswered, waking no responsive echo across the multitudinous corridors of night, the toad makes up his mind to leave the garden. Led by a dowser's instinct, he crosses the accustomed outer boundaries of his habits and hunting rituals, into the unfamiliar.

He is now forging ahead in a direction known only to himself. He moves on through the grass, along rabbit tracks and twisting paths made by shrews, under vaults of pitch darkness, across cold corridors where the sun's rays do not penetrate. Down these sunken roads he goes, confident he won't be noticed, with his sturdily determined, solid, heavy gait, his ungainly gait. Occasionally he pauses to gather in and expel air through his pores; he may break his fast with a few insects, but does not linger over the pleasure. He acts as though this particular pleasure had had to be sacrificed so he could meet an obligation, and he was rather annoyed about it, but what does an appetite for insects matter, when your mind is on more momentous business? Though he retains his imperturbable, taciturn manner, something tremendous is stealthily undermining his senses. He spends a brief digestive interval sitting up on his folded rear legs. He gazes, observes, and considers, looking for the gap in the inextricable tangle of stems and stalks; he gazes till he feels oppressed. Then he sets off again, head down, shoving the undergrowth aside.

Arriving from every direction, they return to the aquatic haunts of childhood, to the glaucous depths of appearances and the undefined shinings of a world beyond. The first comers signal others in the vicinity, using a sequence of short, flowing notes. Some of them take to the water, where they swim with a supple, diamond-wise stretching out and pulling in of the legs, as though to get back in touch with the fluid mystery of their origins. They wish these gathering places were known to none but themselves, so they could mate in pleasurable privacy and not have to worry afterward about raids on their eggs. Most of the time, what they are dealing with is a pool or pond, but in the arid causse country, where limestone does not retain the water brought by rain showers, they may have to settle for the mirrored surface of a disused outdoor public washhouse, or a long puddle, or even, if there's really nothing else near by, a simple wet patch, bordered by reeds and marsh marigolds, at a depression or hollow in the terrain.

Each of them is privately hoping to be fulfilled in the comforting coarseness of genuine lovemaking. But it's easy to make mistakes in the dark, and as their relatively primitive urge is under the control of highly excited senses, they show no discernment in their choice of partner. Anything that moves and looks roughly the right shape there in the shadows, they grab, locking indiscriminately onto male or female.

One of them, approaching his task with a clumsy eagerness that can only be described as stiff and jerky, suddenly feels himself being given a hard time, jolted and shaken up by the partner he is straddling. He tightens his hold, gets a better grip and, if necessary, moves farther up along the other's back, the immediate effect of this surly resistance being in some obscure way to increase his desire.

That is when the male who is bearing the brunt of the attack, rather than waiting for the other fellow to become even more daring in his advances, forcefully expresses his indignation with a few brief, metallic notes, signifying something like "Get off my back! Now!" or "Fuck off, buster!" Upon hearing this clear, unequivocal demand, the disconcerted top toad at once relaxes his hold.

Such episodes are a source of harassment, apprehension, anxiety, outrage, and cold sweat. They bring convulsions to the toadish soul and freeze the fervor of the flesh—but toads are not by nature inclined to feel disappointment or even to consider feeling it. Without grasping what it is that has just occurred, and might well occur again, the confused but well-meaning toad moves aside to try elsewhere.

Finally he has the good fortune to mount a female. This, it immediately appears, is a toad of a different color: softer to the touch, with rounded corners, a satiny moistness, and at the same time a docile, even submissive posture. After several rather trying mistakes and misadventures, the novelty and comfort of the present encounter are most welcome to the male. But it will not do to let his vigor be blunted by a kind of premature appeasement or sudden relaxation.

Beneath him, the female remains still and flattened, motionless and heavy, as though she were trying to hide from an unspecified danger or had opted to do her marital duty without flinching. The male with his forceful nature immediately reacts to her motionless timidity by taking control of the situation. Encouraged by the female's implied consent, he grips her firmly, most often under her armpits, and clasps her in the only mating position that toads have ever dreamt up or authorized, called amplexus.

Alas! Though fervor he may feel, he is unprovided with any organ for copulation. When it's time for love, he does not have the tool for the job: no "penis" for amplexus. The female remains calm, perhaps a shade more confident, and hollows her back just a bit. The male gets even more carried away by these vague promises, and without pausing to reflect on the sorry quality of his pleasure, goes into a cumbersome dance barely punctuated by a few spasms. The female needs this whole series of squeezes if she is to succeed in moving the eggs out of her cloaca.

From the moment egg laying begins, the male forms a double arch with his back legs; he receives the eggs inside the arch, fertilizing them as they come. Gelatinous strings form and swell around the eggs, supporting them on cushions of soft rollers, each roller pierced with a black dot. A potent gel of spheres is formed, the euphoric ovoid expression of an increasingly populous cluster of eggs.

Fertilization in this case is external, but how can we tell whether the love process likewise builds up entirely "outside"? Could the male's pleasure lie solely in the act of *gripping* and in raptures that have no organ for their outlet? And the female's pleasure, merely in the relief of discharging her eggs? Or, in the act of mating, does their union knit bonds not perceptible to us?

Their weddings see the clock go at least once completely around and are accompanied by a single mysterious tinkling. It is a clear, resonant, indeed liquid song, of separate, nearly similar notes, like the concentric, far-off sound of a little bell in a temple beneath the sea. Witchcraft waits in the wings.

The Glass Snake

S uddenly he's there. Your gaze is transfixed, absorbed, held by something coiling and shining, a sinuous flow of mercury or liquid silver. It's a slowworm, a "glass snake." It seems a precious bauble fallen out of the sky, a necklace out of nowhere, dropped, perhaps, by an enchanted being.

When you meet the unexpected, when the unforeseen offers you such a gift as this, you are taken aback. Short-circuited. Dumbfounded. Your eyes are riveted. Your knees buckle. There's nothing left in the world except that slowworm. Everything around him exists only to show him off in a burst of glory. It's as though from now on he must be the sole point of departure for our every thought, or as though he was going to lay down a pattern of behavior for us to follow or be the bearer of a Message.

Something magical has taken place. Fascination keeps us glued to the spot. And we experience yet again the abrupt revelation that somewhere there is always a boundary between what is ordinary and what isn't. An undefined, permanently invisible frontier between the humdrum and the awesome, the usual and the new, utter banality and utter enchantment. It's hard to know where we may find this frontier, which exists nowhere and everywhere at once, all the time and never. And occasionally our confusion is such that we are left wondering where we are in relation to the frontier, which side of it we are on.

To be a slowworm means, first of all, having to be satisfied with a body like a rope tether. You have to stretch out long and narrow, then wiggle into a smooth, scaly sheath. The sheath has the lustrous gray of new pewter, but there is nothing cold about it; on the contrary, touch a slowworm and you will find that he radiates a gentle, silky warmth.

His body conformation is rather unusual. It presents convenient features and amenities, plus a certain freedom of movement, but also a number of major drawbacks. Various permanent frustrations might even result. For the fact is that with no arms and legs, nor any chance of waking up one day to find that he has sprouted a set of them, the slowworm cannot hope ever to hold something in his grasp, or ever to feel, test, and truly experience the texture of things. There are sensations he will never have. An entire province of the unknown, though accessible to other senses, must forever remain closed to him. It is not the slowworm's business, however, to dream of being something other than what he is. His placidness and peace of mind, which do allow for pleasures suited to his situation, no doubt depend on disciplined acceptance of his own nature. A pair of keen orangy eyes, like sulfur tips, enable him to keep vigilant, inquisitive watch over his world at all times.

His comings and goings are effected through a series of intertwined movements plus a narrow range of curves and meanders, but he does not really manage to slither against the grain of the ground beneath him. Unlike the snake flowing through leaves of grass with perfect, sinuous ease, the slowworm, despite his elegant figure, is stiff and awkward as he goes from place to place. When he flees, there are broken angles to his movement. So might we imagine a lizard who has had his legs cut off: he still crawls along, but now with clumsy labored zigzags.

After exploring new territory awhile, with time set aside for rests or pauses when he looks at the world and perhaps recreates it in his own image, the slowworm feels a twinge of hunger. His chosen prey has the same lazy locomotion as himself: small slugs and earthworms are preferred. To appease his hunger, he is equipped with keen, sharp teeth curved backward, so that he can go through a layer of mucus and disembowel his prey or, to be more exact, swallow it unceremoniously, in gluttonous progression. The slug froths in response to the bites, and this slightly salty foam just makes it more delectable. The very elasticity of the muscle is like subtle chewy resistance, and the slowworm goes about his task with increased zeal. He swallows the whole creature. Then he buries himself more or less out of sight to enjoy a digestive nap, while on every hand the summer gives off spicy odors and displays plants maturing or going to seed in a shimmer of pale gold.

At moments of danger, he possesses a surprising special faculty. As soon as he feels anything seize his body, he snaps in two like a necklace. To be very precise, his skeleton is constructed in such a way that it can break off at certain points along the vertebrae, allowing him to get away, leaving the predator utterly bewildered, even stupefied at the humiliating disappointment of being left with nothing but an inert fragment clutched in its claws or fangs. As for the slowworm, he has used the diversion to slide under the grass and out of sight. The cut bleeds hardly at all, quickly forming a healing scar, and a new stump of tail soon grows at the break. That is the second special privilege granted him by his nature, and one in which he can only rejoice. For after all, there would be small glory in venturing out along the paths of love with one section of you missing—not that there aren't certain females with a penchant for compassion and a desire to make themselves indispensable, who would give priority to the male with a handicap, the amputee, the hero who has escaped a deadly peril.

Most of the time, the slowworm braves the world alone. He sets out on solitary errands as the result of a personal, individual decision; when he ventures forth, when he strays abroad, he does it by himself. (He appreciates group living only during hibernation. Then he withdraws with many others of his kind into underground cavities. The biggest slowworms will be found in the farthest recesses, presumably because they were the first arrivals.)

In the season of desires, a female and male are observing one another from a distance, as though to gauge, in one final moment of caution and fright, the joy to be had from this particular embrace. They take their time looking each other over in detail: sheathed body, quicksilver sheen, dark gray back, lighter-colored stomach area. Their keen, orangy eyes meet and glance away; their gazes avoid each other, then meet again, becoming more animated each time. The sky comes tumbling down, smeared in blue, with thick, foamy clouds, broad brushstrokes ending in streaks of white or blue. Then the sky changes color, shifting to darkish gray against which clouds stand out with grays that are darker still. The wind is back in the trees and now the sky shifts once again and clears, without there having been a storm.

Acting upon mutual assent, the slowworms have moved closer to each other in a few sparkling twists. The male takes the female by the nape of the neck, in the sure, keen grip of his teeth, but this time he goes about it with a delicate nibble which, though tender, effectively sharpens her senses. As attraction grows, so does inspiration. He knows instinctively and immediately what expert position to assume, what kind of intertwining is called for; he even considers a whole series of specialized erotic movements. Perhaps both partners have privately and separately prepared for this moment. Perhaps there were wild, ethereal imaginings; safe, comforting dreams; treasures of make-believe; even a confused impression that they were letting their individual beings dissolve to vanish voluptuously in time and space.

Certainly all those "stiff, awkward movements" have disappeared. Their bodies seem shinier, as though lovemaking had fused them for all time. The male bends and curves his body round the body of his chosen bride, tracing a series of semispirals, and repeating the sequence several times over.

From the scales covering their bodies, the light of early summer draws metallic glints, fleeting flashes of iridescent glass. They pursue their undertaking with all due self-abandon and conviction, as though nothing and no one were there to watch them or the presence of a witness didn't matter anyway, so full are they of themselves and their task. They have been tossed up on a far shore where no hunger concerns them any longer, save only the encompassing hunger for the mate.

You really can't help but envy the convenience, when nuptial embraces are in season, of having smooth cylindrical bodies enabling the owners to touch at every point and from every point, roll freely and fluidly over one another and truly intertwine the whole length of their naked bodies without someone's arm or kneecap getting in the way.

During the coupling of the slowworms, everything happens in a subtle series of interlacing, intertwining movements, a long, languid, supple undulation. Curving still more, the male seeks to press his genital organ against the love-partner's organ from underneath, hold that position for a long interval and weld himself to her as though by suction, so that the astonishing act of fertilization may be accomplished.